Surf the Woods™

THE ORDINARY MAN'S TRAIL MAP
TO THE EXTRAORDINARY LIFE

TrailblazeNow

Scripture quotations marked (NIV) are taken from the *Holy Bible, New International Version*®, *NIV*®. Copyright © 1973, 1978, 1984, 2011 by Biblica, Inc.™ Used by permission of Zonderman. All rights reserved worldwide.

Scripture quotations marked (NASB) are taken from the *New American Standard Bible*®. Copyright © 1960, 1962, 1963, 1968, 1971, 1972, 1973, 1975, 1977, 1995 by The Lockman Foundation. Used by permission.

Scripture quotations marked (NLT) are taken from the *Holy Bible, New Living Translation*. Copyright © 1996, 2004, 2007 by Tyndale House Foundation. Used by permission of Tyndale House Publishers, Inc., Carol Stream, Illinois 60188. All rights reserved.

Scripture quotations marked (ESV) are taken from the *Holy Bible, English Standard Version*. Copyright © 2000, 2001 by Crossway Bibles, a division of Good News Publishers. Used by permission. All rights reserved.

Scripture quotations marked (HCSB) are taken from the *Holman Christian Standard Bible*®. Copyright © 1999, 2000, 2002, 2003, 2009 by Holman Bible Publishers. Used by permission. Holman Christian Standard Bible®, Holman CSB®, and HCSB® are federally registered trademarks of Holman Bible Publishers.

Diagram on page 106 is based on registered trade marks belonging to Stephen Covey. His principles are protected intellectual property and feature strongly in the Franklin Covey organization's portfolio of products and services. www.franklincovey.com

ISBN 978-0-9892618-0-7

Published by TrailblazeNow™
400 Casey Drive, Maumelle, AR 72113

Book Design: Sara Condren and Scott Masters

Printed in the United States of America
Second Printing, 2013

www.SurftheWoods.com

*To Courtney, Heather, Brady, Chase, Mary, and Sara,
for rallying around me as I pursued the dream of
writing* Surf the Woods.

CONTENTS

ACKNOWLEDGMENTS

Thanks to…

Dave Tarpley for all those fabulous coaching sessions in which many of the concepts in this book were birthed.

My business partner, Scott Masters, and the fellow team members of Ink Custom Tees for carrying the load while I pursued this project as well as many of my other adventures.

Jacob Schimmel, Kyle Hollaway, Dan Halberg, Steve Campbell, Danny Jones, Chris Sims, Alan Hoffler and the board of TrailblazeNow who are helping me carry this message to men across the country.

Tim Grissom, Sara Condren, Scott Masters and Judy Cook for the countless hours spent editing, designing and shaping this book.

PLAN AMBITIOUSLY

Wake Up the Sleeping Giant

Wake up! Get out of bed. God wants to change the world through your life if you'll just do something.

—Erwin McManus

It was 6:10 p.m., and I was the last person at the office. That's not often the case anymore though working late used to be a way of life for me. But on this particular evening, the quietness of the building puts me in a reflective mood and I begin to stroll through the warehouse.

What a journey it has been. I had started this business twenty-four years earlier on a $5,000 loan from my grandfather. It seems like just yesterday that I sat in a chair across from him and laid out my vision for world t-shirt domination. Unfortunately, I burned through that $5,000 in a matter of months and then moved on to credit cards and cash advances.

Finding a chair, I sit down and begin to relive those early days. At twenty-three and newly married, I had quit my job to start Ink Custom Tees. My vision was to put a t-shirt on the back of every college kid in the country. I smile at the memories of my tiny 10-foot by 10-foot office space, the first t-shirt order I sold, and the trip to Dallas to purchase my first press. Yes, those were happy times, but not easy ones.I hold back a sense of pride that starts to sweep over me by focusing on the realization that God has guided and sustained me on this journey. *It hasn't been my wisdom and leadership skills that have moved me ambitiously through life. It's something much more basic.*

Looking around at that moment, I am surrounded by heavy machinery that's used to create the fabulous t-shirts we sell, each machine an indication of our company's progress and growth. And I tell myself again that I am living a dream. I wonder, *Why don't more people live their dreams? Is there some magic recipe one has to follow that will take him down the road to success?*

I don't think so, at least not in my case. I tried the standard success recipe. I graduated from the University of Arkansas with a degree in business. As a young entrepreneur, each year I read the latest books on business and leadership. I listened to motivational speakers and tried to follow the teachings of great leaders like Dale Carnegie and John Maxwell. But looking back I realize that while all those things played a minor role in my success, it was something more basic that fueled my achievements.

This "something" was given to me by God, and what is so wonderful is that this quality is available to everyone. There's no special skill needed, no school you must attend, nor special process to remember in order to make sure you use it effectively. The quality that has fueled my success is *stubborn determination.*

I have experienced many low points on my entrepreneurial journey, yet it has been my unwillingness to quit that I believe has distinguished my progress from that of many would-be visionaries. Five years after starting Ink, the IRS put tax liens on my house and my business. Being several months behind on sales tax payments to the State of Arkansas, I was under threat of being shut down. I was continually fighting overdrafts with the bank on my business checking account, and the bank was discussing foreclosure. My primary vendors were no longer willing to extend credit terms to me but instead required me to pay cash on delivery. I bounced paychecks, vendor checks, and tax checks. I had extended all my personal credit cards to their limits to the point that I had no reserve. Many people were encouraging me to cut my losses and go bankrupt.

I can remember pulling away from my house each morning on the way to the office completely drained from the stress I was under. I couldn't even face the pressure unless I stopped by the nearby park, pulled out my Bible, and spent a few moments reading and praying just so I could get the courage to walk through the door and into my problems. I did my best to hide the stress from my employees for fear they might quit if they knew the extent of our problems.

Then, one day my assistant walked into my office just before closing time and told me that she had made a mistake in the check register; we had a negative balance of $23,000. The fact that we had no cash was not surprising, but to be $23,000 in the hole was a little much to stomach. To make matters worse, I had a $20,000 payroll to meet the very next day. I left the office ready to call it quits. As I looked at my wife and two young kids that evening, I wrestled inside with feelings of letting my family down. Late into the night I prayed for a miracle, and it came in the form of a dream.

Running Home

In my dream, the scene was like something out of an apocalyptic film. The earth appeared to be destroyed. All the buildings had collapsed to the ground, victims of a nuclear disaster. Smoke was rising from the earth and hidden among the devastation were hideous creatures ready to kill.

On a hill away from this devastation was a secure, white castle surrounded by a moat. I was inside the castle along with the other warriors resting up for battle. Each day the drawbridge would lower, and I, along with the other warriors, would spill out into this hostile landscape and battle with the creatures until nightfall. That's when the drawbridge would lower, and we would run back to the castle to get bandaged up for the battles we would face again the next day. My life was this dream. But at that moment, I could not get back to the castle. I was stranded among the devastation and alone.

When I awoke I walked to the kitchen table and wrote these words.

Running Home

I hear the sounds of distant wars. The cries draw ever near.
As darkness sets around my path, my mind is filled with fear.
I shelter from the evening mist by crouching to the ground.
The cold sinks deep inside my skin. Again I hear the sound.
Screams of pain, a battle cry; they paralyze my soul.

I turn to face the righteous camp, for now I'm running home.

Bombs, they blast around my path as Satan's troops close in.
I fall down to the battlefield. My strength is growing thin.
The enemy moves in to kill. I call out to the Lord.

With one last desperation cry, I brace to feel the sword.
I close my eyes. The moments pass. A silence fills my ears.
And rising up to look around, my eyes are filled with tears.
For on each side surrounding me, angelic forces stand.
And from their midst my Lord appears, and reaches out his hand.

I sat at the kitchen table after writing those words and said to myself, *I am not alone. I can't quit. No matter what anyone says, no matter the hardships, I am going to be an example of determination.*

Emboldened to press forward in my journey, I walked into work a new man the following day. No miracle check arrived in the mail to bail me out of my problems, but I managed through that financial difficulty. I survived that near failure and have survived others on my way to building and sustaining a quality business in central Arkansas. The ups and downs have all been a part of living my dream, and they have only helped to strengthen my resolve.

You Can Live Your Dream Now

It is time to stop listening to the come-back-to-reality, safe thinkers all around us that have somehow been given the label of wise. Aspiring to a life where you try to avoid adversity by having safe goals, getting a safe job, building up a safe retirement, and living in a safe neighborhood is not the path to an abundant life at all. In fact, I would argue that it is a slow, sad, and boring road to death. Real wisdom comes when you take seriously what the Bible says about the Power that resides within you and what that Power wants to do through you if you have the courage to follow.

I'm not referring to a plan for wealth. I'm talking about living a life that is truly satisfying.

I wrote this book with the idea of giving the everyday man and woman, just like you and me, some renewed hope that the dreams we once aspired to can become reality. In fact, it doesn't need to be some far-off reality. With the principles laid out in this book, you can start living your dream now. All that is needed are the guts to begin dreaming again and the will to take those first steps away from the safe life. Don't think that I'm talking about dreaming in a soft, fantasyland kind of way. I'm referring to a concrete understanding that God created you for a specific purpose. God gave you specific skills, abilities, and desires, and He wills to use those skills, abilities, and desires for His purposes. The great thing is, God's purposes are extraordinary. They are the kind of purposes you dream about being involved in, ambitious purposes that most never have the courage to pursue. I call these ambitious purposes our *God-inspired dreams.*

God-Inspired Dreams: The ambitious pursuits God specifically calls you toward in partnership with His unlimited power

We all admire the inspiring stories of the everyday man or woman who had a dream. Against all odds, they rose above the naysayers, stayed the course, survived the adversity, and saw their dream become reality. Many times we put these individuals in a special category apart from us by saying that they caught a break in the pursuit of their dream or they had abilities that very few people have. Both of those statements are true about successful dreamers. But the same can be true of you when you begin pursuing your own God-inspired dream. Throughout this book, I will lay out the principles I use daily that have helped me and those I have coached to live out our personal and professional dreams. I will illustrate those principles with the many adventures that have been my teachers. I believe you will find that these simple principles will revolutionize the way you live, and they will make living life a fantastic and exciting adventure.

The story of my life is summed up in the Bible verse 2 Corinthians 12:9 (NIV): " 'My grace is sufficient for you, for my power is made perfect in weakness.' Therefore I will boast all the more gladly about my weaknesses, so that Christ's power may rest on me."

Mine is the story of an ordinary man who through God's power has had the privilege to do some extraordinary things. I hope you enjoy the read. More importantly, I hope it helps put you on the path to living your own God-inspired dreams.

CHAPTER ONE

Rise Above the Practical

Plan Ambitiously

We try to be too reasonable about what we believe. What I believe is not reasonable at all. In fact, it's hilariously impossible. Possible things aren't worth much. These crazy impossible things keep us going.

—Madeleine L'Engle

July 2009: I was standing at an altitude of nearly 17,000 feet above sea level as I lowered my backpack to the ground and grinned. My expedition's partners in turn lowered their heavy packs and we gave a round of high fives. We were getting closer to proving once and for all that there was a large man-made structure underneath the snow

19

and ice near the summit of Mount Ararat in Turkey. It had been a long, ambitious journey that brought me to this point, and I wanted to relish every moment. I was accompanying a team consisting of an archeologist, a geologist, a couple of American men with local connections, some Kurdish porters, and a fellow mountain climber. We were nearing the location where we planned to dig for the remains of Noah's ark. If the satellite readings had been interpreted properly, we were close. But weeks of work lay ahead.

My experience in wilderness navigation, alpine climbing, and wilderness medicine had caught the attention of the expedition leader, Richard Bright. But as I looked around that day, I still had to pinch myself. These guys were experts in their fields, and I was a nobody by comparison. There were plenty of other candidates more qualified to keep others alive on this snow-covered rock pile. What had brought me here was the willingness to dream big, coupled with the stubborn determination to make my dream a reality.

This was the perfect adventure for me. Everything about the experience meshed with my passion, strengths, and life story. My passion for wilderness adventure started when I was a young boy. I spent countless hours exploring the woods near my home in Arkansas. My favorite memories as a kid were of camping with family and friends in the Ozark Mountains. Camping then led to backpacking, which in turn led to climbing and caving. Climbing and caving opened the door to mountaineering. Eventually, all those experiences pushed me to test my survival skills by spending four weeks alone in the largest wilderness area in the south central United States.

I had survived harsh conditions as an entrepreneur and as an outdoorsman, but so far Mount Ararat was the most dangerous adventure I had taken on. Mount Ararat is located in a very remote part of Turkey. It is a volcanic mountain, which is snowcapped year round. The foothills of the mountain spill over into Iran to the east and Armenia to the north. It takes military permission to access the mountain because of the danger of crossing paths with gun-toting freedom fighters called the PKK (English translation: Kurdistan Workers' Party). This Kurdish army inhabits the mountain and they will steal, kill, and destroy if they believe it will further their cause of liberty within the Turkish borders. As an outdoorsman, a little danger energizes me, but this was truly the first time I had experienced the very real possibility of being caught in the crossfire of bullets.

None of the danger mattered at that moment. There I was, standing on top of the mountain where I believed civilization was given a second chance. To have the opportunity to work in partnership with God to reveal to the world the reality of Noah's ark, I was living my dream!

Dreamer's Principle 1: Plan Ambitiously

Inside each one of us, deep in the recesses of our soul, is a special room. This room is filled with the wonderful thoughts about what we hope to achieve with our life. It houses the great thoughts we have about our strengths and our potential, as well as our goals and dreams. There is no place here for mediocrity or negativity. At times we may allow others access to this room by sharing our treasured thoughts with them, but more often than not, those individuals rain negativity on our dreams because their misery wants our company. Every time we risk talking about our dreams, we risk hearing about how that dream won't work or that dream isn't practical. Sometimes it may just be a nonverbal clue like a smirk or maybe a small chuckle. Every time this occurs, the door to our dreams shuts just a little.

Sometimes we may take a risk and act upon those dreams. Frequently, things don't go as expected and we suffer a letdown, setback, or even a defeat. As a result, we often get hurt. And to make matters worse, there are always spectators that witness our struggles.

Spectators tend to enjoy making sarcastic comments from the sidelines as they laugh about our failures. They may not laugh out loud, but we know by their countenance what they are saying: "Get back to reality. That was a silly idea anyway." And again, our dream door shuts a little more. Eventually, it may shut completely. What was once a wonderful part of who we are is now a dark room shut tight by pain and hurt. We bury our dreams and have trouble accessing them ever again. We need a *dream-door opener.*

As a business leader, church leader, and life coach, I try to be a dream-door opener for others. I have sat across the desk from many individuals over the years who are frustrated with life. For one reason or another, things are not going as they had planned. They may articulate the reasons differently, but from my experience, the path to their disappointment has a common theme in most cases. Somewhere along their life journey, they closed the door to their dreams and settled for the path to security, a more comfortable path where no one ever questioned or challenged them.

Just by asking a simple question I can learn a lot about how far off path an individual is in their life journey, and how hard it's going to be to inspire that individual back on the path toward victory. I often ask, "What are the dreams you have for your life?" And I am always astonished how hard it is for people to talk about that subject. It's almost as if working toward an ambitious life goal is as much a fantasy as believing in Santa Claus. Conversely, people generally seem to view ambition as a safe place to better order their life. Ask someone their dreams, and they often reply, "I'd like to get to a place where I'm healthy and have a good job so that I'm able to live a comfortable life." But do we honestly believe God calls us to that kind of dream in partnership with His unlimited power? Why not instead dream about changing the world with our lives?

As a life coach, when I sit down with a person, I try to keep in mind that God created this person and has a wonderfully ambitious plan for his life. God also has unlimited power in order to carry out His plans in partnership with those who follow hard after His leadership. The Bible says in 2 Chronicles 16:9 (NASB), "The eyes of the LORD move to and fro throughout the earth that He may strongly support those whose heart is completely His." God is looking for people who will wholeheartedly give themselves to His plan for their lives. And you know where those plans are found? Often they are locked away inside that cobweb-filled dream room that was locked shut some years earlier. It's time we cracked that door open again.

Effective Dreamers

When I press people to talk about their life dreams, I have found that they tend to fall into five categories. About 25 percent say they just want a comfortable life. These people are what I call *safe-zoners*. They can still be rescued from the slow, boring path leading to a disappointing life, but first they need help getting back on the path to an inspiring life. I seek to move them forward in their journey by helping them unlock their dream door once again.

Another 25 percent can talk on and on about their dreams, but they are hardly any closer to living them than the day their vision began. These people are what I call *wanderers*. They are easier to rescue, because they have wide-open dream doors. They just have trouble putting legs to their vision. I use the elements outlined in the coming chapters of this book to help them move their vision further down the road to reality.

Then there are the 25 percent that when pressed can articulate their dreams, but they have all kinds of reasons as to why they aren't moving those dreams along. I call these people excuse makers. They are a little harder to reach because they tend to have a problem accepting responsibility for where they are in life. When you talk to these people, they say success comes to those who receive breaks that they never received or have talents they don't have. Some say they are just too busy with life to pursue dreams. It takes much persistence and coaching to bring these people along in the journey.

Then there are the 20 percent I call *disbelievers*. They tell me that dreamers are immature. They talk about dreamers as people that need to get back on the road to reality. When I encounter someone like this, I don't spend any energy trying to inspire him or her. I coach safe-zoners, wanderers, and even (somewhat reluctantly) excuse makers. About the only thing that can be done for a disbeliever is to pray they bump up to being an excuse maker. At least then they will still have a chance to live their dream.

Finally, there is a handful in every hundred that I call *effective dreamers*. These are the few that are effectively living their dreams as they move through their everyday lives. Not all of them have reached the pinnacle of their dreams and goals, but they are effectively moving their God-sized aspirations along in a systematic and consistent manner. They have a clear understanding of how God has uniquely designed them for a compelling purpose. They are aiming toward that purpose, and they are consistently taking steps toward their dream.

No doubt, some effective dreamers were born with a silver spoon in their mouth, but not all. In fact, most of these people have normal jobs, normal homes, and normal families. What's not normal is the joy they experience as they live their own unique adventure. They are excited about where they are headed with their life. They love waking up each morning. They have great expectations of what is to come in their lives. They are confident, compelling, and infectiously optimistic. The trouble is there aren't enough of them in this world.

How do you move from just being a dreamer to being an effective dreamer, you ask? Start by learning how to *surf the woods!*

Caffeinated Question

You'll get more out of this book if you'll take the time to discuss it with a trusted friend or two. That's why I'm providing these questions at the end of each chapter. Caffeine is optional.

1. What are your dreams?

2. What makes these dreams important to you?

3. Would you classify yourself currently as safe-zoner, wanderer, excuse maker, disbeliever, or an effective dreamer?

CHAPTER TWO

Surf the Woods

Each man should frame life so that at some future hour, fact and his dream meet.

—Victor Hugo

When I was in my early forties, I decided to put all my wilderness skills to the test in a four-week journey of solitude through the Leatherwood and Lower Buffalo wilderness areas of north central Arkansas. A lifetime of outdoor experience had taught me many useful skills, but I had never taken on anything this rigorous. My goal was to chart forgotten waterfalls, caves, and old homesteads in the largest contiguous wilderness area in the south central United States. It sounds silly now, but at the outset I had visions of beautiful stands of timber that I would stroll through leisurely, taking a break now and then for a nap in a grassy meadow or by a rolling brook. That was far from reality! What I found were primarily tangled webs of thickets and briars with occasional open areas for camping and resting. In many cases, to find the beauty of a vista, cave, or waterfall, I had to blaze a trail through miles and miles of brush.

For the first few days, my strategy for navigating the woods involved finding a location on the topography map that looked inviting. Then I would plug the coordinates into my GPS and begin hacking through brush with my machete. But the trouble with following my GPS in that environment was the constant temptation to watch the directional indicator and blaze a direct trail toward my target location. For hours I would cut my way through the thickets and briars with my machete in one hand while still keeping watch on my GPS in the other. It was a painfully slow process as the thorns sliced my arms and tore holes in my clothes while I inched along. I would spend hour upon hour with this method of breaking trail only to realize that I was making little progress toward my goal and draining myself of energy in the process. If I were going to last four weeks, I had to find a better way to navigate.

One morning, I decided to try something different. As usual, I plugged the coordinates of my target location into my GPS. Then I took a careful look in the general direction I needed to walk. After I was confident of the direction, I fastened the GPS unit to the strap of my backpack and put away my machete. I decided that I would hold my trek poles in my hands that day. Normally used for balance and stability, my trek poles had been strapped to the outside of my pack for most of the journey thus far. I had used them a couple of times for added balance on creek crossings, but I was about to find out that they would serve a much greater purpose.

With my hands free from the GPS and machete, I could keep my head up so that I could better scout the landscape ahead. Without my eyes fastened to the directional arrow of my GPS, I could adjust my path to try and avoid the brush rather than bushwhack through it. Occasionally, I couldn't avoid the heavy brush. On those occasions, I learned to use my trek poles to carefully move the thorns aside so that I could walk through almost any tight spot without tearing my arms to pieces. I unclipped the GPS unit from my backpack strap every hundred yards or so to get another read on the general direction for the next leg of my journey, just in case I had wandered off course. Once I was confident in my direction of travel, I set off again. Before long, I was proficient at this method of blazing trail. I was making quick, efficient, almost effortless progress to my landmarks.

As I lay under the stars a few nights later, I began to think about the trail I was blazing through life. In many ways, it matched my experiences of blazing a trail through the woods. In the wilderness, it had taken a lot of trial and error, much of which was painful and exhausting, to finally discover how I could best traverse the untamed backwoods of Arkansas. Once I had the right tools in my hands, and kept my head up to survey the landscape out in front, the trip became a pleasure rather than a grind. This experience helped change my life, so much so that I nicknamed this method of wilderness travel *surfing the woods.*

Looking up at the stars that evening, I knew that just as there are effective ways to navigate the wilderness, there are also effective methods to navigate toward an abundant life, methods that could be taught using stories from my own journey, lessons I had learned while on adventures in the various aspects of my own life. I wanted to help people live effectively. I wanted to help people surf life.

God-Inspired Dreams

Do you ever feel lost in the wilderness of your life? Maybe you feel that your dreams are dead. Somewhere along the way you may have abandoned dreaming altogether. Now you are just going through the motions with your life, not sure how to navigate effectively. Often, well-intentioned individuals find themselves abandoning their dreams for the security of the safe zone because they can never seem to get anywhere with their ideas. The truth is you may have been just a short distance away from living your dream when you gave up. When I see this situation in an individual that I am coaching, I look for three possible reasons as to why they aren't effectively executing on their dreams.

1. The person's dream isn't God inspired. It doesn't line up with their unique story, strength, and energizing passion; therefore, it's just an idea they have. (I will talk more about this later.) God blesses the path He chooses for your life because it's a work He wants to do and not some winning idea you think you have. As a result, it's critical to find your God-inspired dreams by looking closely at the story of your life and the unique way God designed you. Pursuing your own dreams apart from God's blessing may work for a while, but eventually it won't satisfy.

2. The person may have had a God-inspired dream at one time but encountered some difficultly along the way and abandoned the pursuit.

3. The person has a God-inspired dream but is unclear about how to effectively pursue that dream. Most of these

people I would call wanderers. They need some help moving their dreams along successfully.

To be effective in living our dreams, we need tools. This book and the concepts within it are life-effectiveness tools that help people spring up from the boring monotony of an uninspiring life. They place individuals in the proper position to begin surfing life.

When you're surfing life, you find enjoyment in each day because you're walking the energizing path God prepared for you. The Bible says in Ephesians 2:10 (esv), "For we are His workmanship, created in Christ Jesus for good works, which God prepared beforehand, that we should walk in them." The Bible also tells us in Hebrews 11:6 (niv) that "without faith it is impossible to please God." A life of faith is a life lived apart from the confines of always making safe steps and practical decisions. A person living their God-inspired dream is happy and contented living their life apart from the safe zone.

Take a look at your own life. Are you currently carrying out the great works that God in His unlimited power prepared for you? If we're honest, most of us aren't living the kind of life we aspire to live, nor are we living the life God desires us to live. Most of us are playing it safe. That's why the concepts in this book are so important.

What you will get from *Surf the Woods* is twofold:

1. Insights that may help you discover your unique calling, aligning you with your God-inspired dreams.

2. An ongoing, simple posture of action that will put you in position to begin living your God-inspired dreams.

And just in case you're still not convinced that this book is for you, consider:

- We all have unique stories and experiences.
- We all have strengths.
- We all have energizing passions.
- Deep down, we all want to make a significant impact with our lives.

But most of us feel stuck! I wrote this book to help you get unstuck and moving forward toward a rewarding life. Throughout the remainder of the book, I will give you some insights and thought-provoking questions in order to help you align your life to the powerful and unique dreams God has in store for you. These insights are based on four key elements of effectiveness. These elements I call the 4 Dreamer's Principles. These principles lead to the proper mindset that I believe you must have in order to live your God-inspired dream.

4 Dreamer's Principles

1. Plan Ambitiously

2. Prepare Persistently

3. Persevere Courageously

4. Accelerate Toward Fear

Additionally, I will lay out helpful postures of action that I call the 10 Trailblazer's Rhythms. These insights are taken from my own personal experiences as an adventurer both in the office and on the trail. They are helpful mindsets and routines that set the proper pace for moving effectively along your journey.

10 Trailblazer's Rhythms

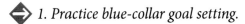 *1. Practice blue-collar goal setting.*

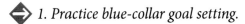 *2. Focus on the next small step.*

 3. Celebrate short-term wins.

 4. Maintain momentum.

 5. Adjust as clarity presents.

 6. Maintain a manageable pace.

 7. Seize the moments.

 8. Don't journey alone.

 9. Overload.

 10. Prioritize paradoxically.

It is an easy thing to be a dreamer; it is far more difficult to walk effectively in your dreams. That is why the 4 Dreamer's Principles and the 10 Trailblazer's Rhythms are so important. If you take seriously the insights in this book, you will begin to see how God has uniquely designed you for works that He prepared specifically for you before you were born.

> For we are His workmanship, created in Christ Jesus for good works, which God prepared beforehand so that we would walk in them. (Ephesians 2:10, NASB)

This book can help you begin living your own fulfilling life. No longer will you sit back watching a select few live their inspiring dreams. You will start feeling the joy and contentment that goes along with living abundantly. You will be *surfing the woods!*

Water's Eyes

A brook leads such a peaceful life.
Never worry, never strife.
It glides along on nature's arm
Exempt from pain, exempt from harm.

The water, on the other hand,
Gets banged around upon the land.
Over rock and over stone,
Giving off a desperate moan.

We see our lives through water's eyes,
Handcuffed to a brook that tries
To push us through a violent course,
A subject to the Power Source.

A brook is what the Father sees,
Giving us a life that frees
Us to rest upon His arm,
Accepting pain. Rejecting harm.

Caffeinated Questions

1. What dreams have you had that you have not executed effectively?

2. Why have you not executed those dreams effectively?

3. Based on your wildest dreams, how might God use you to impact the world?

PREPARE PERSISTENTLY

Blue-Collar Goal Setting

Over-preparation is the foe of inspiration.

—Napoleon Bonaparte

Mount Ararat is the largest mountain in Turkey at nearly 17,000 feet above sea level, consisting of two prominent peaks: the summit and the lesser eastern summit.

Three of us on the advance team had agreed to climb a few days ahead to find the dig location on the eastern plateau and establish camp. We made the slow, arduous climb up to the western plateau along the southern tourist route. The weather had been uncooperative, as often happens at such high altitudes. Freezing wind and snow and colder-than-normal temperatures were taking their toll. My fellow climber, Kevin DeVries, and I were both experienced at alpine climbing in adverse conditions and agreed that the conditions were too dangerous to push farther. We scrambled to set up our tent just below the summit, a couple of hours short of where we had planned to stop. And what we hoped to be just a few hours sheltering from the storm, turned into a couple of days of being trapped in the confines of our tents, waiting for the weather to improve.

Finally, the weather broke. By then, we had expected to be joined by the remaining members of our team. I could only speculate as to why they had not yet arrived. We had no effective way to communicate with those located at the 14,000-foot camp. I presumed that they had decided to wait at the lower camp until the weather improved. Kevin and I discussed our next steps and decided that we would make the two-hour ascent to the eastern plateau in order to pinpoint the location for the team's dig. The plan was to mark the location and then descend back to our current camp and wait for the rest of the team to arrive. Curiosity was killing us. We had waited long enough.

For years before I got formally involved in the search for Noah's ark, I had gathered information on the history of the search. Over the last 100 years there have been many people claim to have located the final resting place of the ark, but no one has produced conclusive, scientific evidence. There have been plenty of eyewitness testimonies of people claiming to have seen the ark on Mount Ararat, but none could produce good pictures or wood samples that prove to be aged appropriately. I questioned whether these claims were fabrications, and I'm convinced most of them are. But if the ark was on Ararat, I wanted to be a part of a team that could finally prove it scientifically. One of the most intriguing things I had read was about a certain man I'll call Mr. X, whose name I'm keeping secret because he doesn't want to be associated with the search.

In the 1980s, Mr. X and one of the advisors to our team, Dr. Don Shockey, had a chance encounter. Mr. X had access to classified satellite technology that was capable of looking underneath the ice on Mount Ararat. He agreed to turn the satellite toward Mount Ararat to see if any remnants of the structure could be found under the ice cap. After a couple of weeks, the men met to discuss the findings. Mr. X confirmed that he had scanned the mountain and found not only one but two very large man-made objects about 1,000 feet apart underneath the ice cap on Ararat. They appeared to have once been connected to each other because there was a line of debris that connected them. They were completely covered in ice; therefore, they couldn't be detected by any visual scan of the mountain. He said he was confident they were not rock or ice but were man-made. In his professional opinion, they were probably wood.

It had been twenty years since those findings, and this expedition was the first time Turkey had allowed a fully equipped team access to the eastern plateau to dig for these objects. I reached deep inside my backpack and felt for my portable GPS unit. Pulling it out, Kevin and fellow climber Eric Ream looked on as I programmed in the confidential coordinates Mr. X had given us. Ferocious winds blew stinging snow against our faces as we stood near the tents, preparing for the next leg of the journey. I pushed "GOTO" on my GPS unit and set forth in pursuit of what many believe could be the greatest archeological find of all time.

As Kevin and Eric followed my footsteps across the snow, I remember thinking that I was blazing a trail toward a part of the mountain few had ever reached. The risk was great as we left the southern tourist route and the protection of the Turkish military safe-zone. Guerrilla forces had easy access to this portion of the mountain and were unfriendly to projects the Turkish military supported.

We skirted the summit of Ararat by taking a more direct route along the northern face of the mountain. It was slow going as we made our way toward the eastern plateau. After about an hour, the eastern summit finally came into view. I knew that the dig location was now less than an hour away. We strapped on our crampons and pulled out our ice axes for the final push. I'll never forget the moment I took that step up and caught sight of the eastern plateau. It was highly emotional. I was nearing the place where civilization began again. I unclipped my GPS unit from the strap of my backpack and focused on the screen; I was less than 700 feet away from the coordinates.

As we continued to push ever closer to the goal, I reflected on what had brought me to this moment. I was just an average guy with no special credentials to put me in this position. I wasn't a true professional mountain climber. I wasn't an archeologist or a scientist. No one I knew was acquainted with anyone that had ever been part of a team searching for the ark. In fact, most people I knew laughed at the idea of me going off in search of Noah's ark. I had no contacts in Turkey that could put me in a position for this search. I had never even been out of the United States. For crying out loud, I ran a small business in Arkansas making custom imprinted t-shirts! Just a couple of weeks before I was sweating like crazy in the back of my warehouse as I printed t-shirts with my crew. It seemed miraculous that I was even here, but I had put myself in this position by listening to God's call and maximizing my God-given strengths and passions. Now, Mr. Ordinary was about to do something extraordinary.

I watched as the distance on my GPS screen continue to shrink: 300 feet . . . 200 feet . . . 100 feet . . . bull's-eye! My eyes welled up with tears as I buried my ice ax deep in the snow directly over the target. I was standing directly over the final resting place of Noah's ark.

I have set out to accomplish some fairly high goals in my life. Not all of those goals have turned out the way I had envisioned them. Some have been successes and some, failures. But all of those goals started out with one thing—an idea that had very little long-term planning. I know that sounds like a bad idea, but hear me out.

Finding the final resting place of Noah's ark was not my first ambitious dream; starting my own business at the age of twenty-three was. After all this time, leading my business is still a daily adventure. I am constantly faced with new challenges that grow my leadership muscles and force me to be creative. I have learned more about perseverance and leadership as a business owner than in any other aspect of my life.

Several years ago, I could tell that the culture of my business wasn't what I desired it to be. I had a set of core values, but they were not being embraced. In fact, I could see how the atmosphere was lowering productivity, hindering creativity, and leading to lower profits. I needed change, but it was going to have to come not just from me, but also from my core leaders. It would require measurable goal-setting practices. With my leadership style (inspirational), the goal-setting system would have to be easy; and a simple system of "inspecting what is expected" was going to be the key. Otherwise, my leaders would not embrace it, and I would have trouble enforcing it.

Working with my personal life coach, Dave Tarpley, my leadership team and I began asking ourselves what questions would really need to be answered each week in order to bring small incremental changes which could lead to big results over time. We came up with three questions that are so simple they're almost laughable, but the results were amazing. Every other week I had a focus meeting with my leaders individually and I asked them to fill out a simple document that centered on these three questions. What one or two things do I need to (1) start doing, (2) stop doing, and (3) keep doing in order to bring about the desired results and embrace Ink's core values? Those simple questions revolutionized the focus of our meetings and generated simple action points that began changing Ink's culture for the better in just a matter of months. We called it *Blue-Collar Goal Setting*.

Trailblazer's Rhythm 1: Practice Blue-Collar Goal Setting

Blue collar goal setting takes what most people see as an intangible, subjective process and makes it doable for the average guy. No need for a Harvard business degree with this approach. I have found standard goal-setting methods mentally draining. The average results-driven leader rarely wants to slow down and go through the process often enough to be effective. People who spend time writing one-, three-, and five-year plans often have trouble adjusting those plans as new information presents itself, or as unexpected ideas emerge.

The tendency of standard goal setting approaches is to be locked in to what could be outdated ideas or concepts that might have made sense the month prior, but could be slightly irrelevant today. With blue-collar goal setting you can easily adjust plans when needed. The three simple "stop-start-keep" questions I just mentioned automatically break goals down into very small steps that are quickly attainable, and as a result, generate quick momentum. People see weekly results, and those results pay big dividends over time. Keeping it simple helps you keep achieving.

I have noticed some trends as I watch people start to embrace the principles I teach and begin walking their unique dream journey. Most seem to get good initial traction, but then their momentum slows when they start to encounter obstacles and challenges that require endurance. It's the persevering legs of the dream journey where people tend to give out and seek refuge in the safe zone. Often times, they encounter an obstacle that they cannot seem to work around, so they give up. These are occasions where blue-collar goal setting can make the difference between breaking through to new horizons or calling it quits.

I have found that people must become proficient at managing three core issues in order to be successful and surf life effectively during the enduring phases of their own ambitious dream journey. There are other issues as well, but most other issues can be grouped underneath these three:

Managing self
Managing relationships
Managing problems and opportunities

When I noticed that the culture of my business had changed for the worse, I was almost ready to sell the company and move on. I was walking a persevering leg of my dream journey at Ink. In order to change the culture, I felt that I needed to start by defining what a good team member's work habits and interactions look like. After all, the benchmark must be identified if you want people to know what is expected of them.

These benchmark, cultural values became known in my company as the "Ink Way." I have listed these cultural values below strictly for the purpose of illustrating my point on blue-collar goal setting.

THE !nk WAY™

Manage Self
- Start Prompt, Finish Strong
- You are Here, You are Needed
- Be a Flexible Expert
- Clean as You Go
- Own Your Mistakes
- Develop Depth

Manage Relationships
  • Applaud and Challenge
  • Stay Connected

Manage Problems and Opportunities
  • Execute ETA (enthusiastically, timely, accurately)
  • Define Problems and Offer Solutions

The leadership team agreed on these values and printed them on laminated cards that could easily fit in our pockets. I gave a copy to each of the employees. The plan was to reinforce the values by publicly praising the employee using the "Ink Way" card whenever we saw the values being embraced. In contrast, an employee was to be privately confronted if they weren't working according to the values.

With this plan in mind, we set out to change the culture of our business with blue-collar goal setting. Each week, we talked in our one-on-one and group meetings about what we needed to start, stop, and keep doing in order to move the company forward culturally and organizationally. Sometimes those answers came easily, just as they will for you as you pursue your God-inspired dreams. Other times, the answers weren't so easy, and we were at a loss to know what to do next. The same thing will happen to you as you follow your dreams. During those difficult times, seek to gain direction by applying blue-collar goal setting in the areas of managing self, managing relationships, and managing problems and opportunities. It will help you to define the problem and generate simple solutions.

As you try to move your dreams forward in your own personal life, it could be that you need to stop spending three hours each night watching TV. You need to start applying the principle of *overload* (discussed in an upcoming chapter) and gradually turn a portion of that TV time into productive time. Perhaps you have been doing great in your efforts to get back in shape physically (managing self), and you want to keep that momentum going. Then ask the same questions regarding relationships, and finally problems and opportunities. Whenever I am stuck, I always start with these three simple stop-start-keep questions in order to generate much needed momentum.

Check out appendix 1 for a simple, yet effective, Blue-Collar Goal Setting worksheet. With this simple goal-setting method, you can turn persevering moments into breakthrough moments, putting your God-inspired dream in motion.

Caffeinated Questions

1. What do you need to stop doing this week to move your dreams forward effectively?

2. What do you need to start doing this week to move your dreams forward effectively?

3. What do you need to keep doing to move your dreams forward effectively?

CHAPTER FOUR

Prepare Persistently

I will prepare and some day my chance will come.

—Abraham Lincoln

I put my shovel down and looked around. I could see some clouds building off to the south. Kevin and I had endured almost a week of this weather. Whiteouts come quickly on Mount Ararat, and I knew trouble could be coming. In a whiteout, one minute you can clearly see what direction you need to walk, and the next minute the snow is so blinding you have to use a GPS or compass in order to navigate safely. It had looked so beautiful earlier that I had foolishly left my GPS and compass at the campsite. How many times was I going to have to learn this lesson the hard way? I thought about retrieving it before the weather got too bad. I could just walk quickly back to the campsite about 100 yards away, grab my GPS unit, and get a reading on the tents. Then I could go back to the dig site and continue working. That way if the weather got bad, we would have no problem locating the tents in the event of a whiteout.

As I looked back at the campsite, I could see the tents clearly. I reasoned that we were so close there was likely no way to get lost, even if the weather deteriorated quickly. Besides, in walking back and forth from the tents to the dig site, we had created a pretty well-defined path. If we were to encounter whiteout conditions, we could just look down and follow that path through the snow back to the tents. So, I picked up the shovel and decided to continue digging.

Dr. Randall Price, another member of our team, had joined Kevin and me. He was an archeologist and a professor at Liberty University. The rest of the team had been unable to reach the dig site. Eric Ream had gone back down the mountain and was headed home to the United States.

We had a lot of work to do and a limited time in which to do it, complicated by the fact that at any moment the Turkish military could revoke our permit and require us to come back down the mountain. Satellite technology had indicated that at its shallowest point the ark was 18 feet underneath the snow and fell off quickly from there. The GPS coordinates took us within a reasonable distance to that shallow point. We had hoped to get in contact with Mr. X once we had placed a few metal snow pickets in the ground. That way, he could get another reading from the satellite to confirm that our location was in fact correct. However, we had been unable to make contact with him, so rather than wait any longer, we made the decision to trust the coordinates and begin the dig.

We got up early and marked a 15-foot by 15-foot outline in the snow, making sure our target coordinates were directly in the center. Kevin and I each carried an alpine shovel in our backpacks. That was our only method for digging at the moment. The rest of the crew was to arrive the next day with more shovels, slam bars, and chainsaws for cutting through the ice. The three of us took turns with the two shovels. It went quickly for the first 4–5 feet down. At that point, we hit ice. The plan was to clear the snow out of the square that day. We would have to wait for the rest of the crew and equipment before trying to excavate the ice from the hole.

The clouds continued to build and within a matter of minutes the snow started falling heavily. I decided it would be best to make a quick run down to the tent. I needed to retrieve the GPS unit in case things got worse. I put the shovel down, told the guys my plan, and started toward the tents. As I walked, the snow got heavier; within a couple of minutes, I could no longer see the tents. I turned around to look for the dig site, and I could no longer see it either. Every direction was a wall of white. I decided to look down at the ground, focusing on the footprints we had left in the snow. I would let them lead me to the tents. What should have taken another two or three minutes was taking far too long. I still couldn't see the tents, and our old footprints were quickly filling up with fresh snow. I stopped and looked intently up ahead. I could barely make out some color against the wall of white. It had to be the tents so I walked toward the color. A few more steps closer and I could see that I was mistaken. It was not the tents but my partners still shoveling away at the dig site. I had gotten so lost that I circled back around to where I had started.

I suggested to the guys that we had better abandon the dig for now and take cover in the tents. We each took turns pointing toward the direction we thought the tents were located. Conditions like this are very disorienting; each one of us had a different opinion as to which way to walk. We stood around for a few minutes debating the proper direction. The conditions were getting worse as the snow seemed to fall even harder, and the wind continued to pick up. These were the perfect conditions for hypothermia: cold, windy, and wet. The safety and warmth of our tents was only 100 yards away, but we had no idea which direction. Out of the corner of my eye, I caught a glimpse of what I thought to be the bright yellow color of one of our tents. We decided to take a chance and head in that direction.

In these kinds of whiteout conditions, there is a real possibility that you can lose sight of one another as you walk and wind up being lost and alone. To prevent that from happening we decided to walk step for step in each other's tracks as we made our way toward the tents. I can remember struggling to walk against the heavy winds and driving snow as it blew ferociously in from the south side of the mountain. We walked for about five minutes when we realized we were lost. We should have been to the tents at that point.

We decided to stop and wait a few minutes to see if we could get a small break in the weather. Just a slight break in the wind might be all we needed to spot the tents. At that point I was concerned that we might be nearing an edge of the plateau where one wrong step could mean falling to our deaths. We huddled close together to try and shield one another from the biting wind. The weather continued to deteriorate. For the first time in my life, I was standing outside watching lightning in a snowstorm. Here we were on the highest point in all of Turkey with thunder and lightning rattling all around us. I learned in Wilderness First Responder School to stay put when you are lost and to separate from others when you are in a lightning storm. By keeping one of the rules, we were in effect breaking both. No way were we going to separate.

As we huddled close together, fully exposed to the storm, we talked about this being the worst conditions any of us had ever experienced. That was pretty impressive especially coming from Kevin. He had climbed Mt. McKinley, the tallest mountain in North America, and had also been on an expedition to the North Pole. Both of those environments were harsh, but he said he had never seen such brutal weather as what we were experiencing at that moment. Fifteen minutes stretched to an hour as we huddled close together waiting for the weather to break. In reality, we were all in the process of freezing to death, and I slowly began to accept the possibility that this was how I might die. I will never forget the sincerity in our words as we each prayed out loud to God for help.

I had been keeping an eye on what I thought was some color about thirty yards to my left. I kept thinking the weather would break any second so I could tell more clearly if the color I was seeing was in fact the tents. We decided we had to take a chance and walk toward the color. The prospect of hypothermia was becoming more and more likely since the weather showed no sign of letting up. We all agreed that moving was our best chance of survival. I led out slowly as the others followed closely in my footsteps. As I walked, the color became more apparent. Thank God! We had found the tents.

I can remember crawling into the warmth of my sleeping bag that day. It had been just moments before that I was pondering the prospect of freezing to death. I thought how ironic that would have been if we would have died in the storm that day. Whoever discovered us would have found us within 100 feet of the life-giving protection of our tents—so close to life, and yet huddled together, dead. I was frustrated with myself. I should have been a little more prepared.

Dreamer's Principle 2: Prepare Persistently

Effective dreamers not only plan ambitiously, they also prepare persistently. To prepare persistently means that you keep moving your God-inspired dreams along incrementally and effectively, even against adversity. This is about gaining and keeping momentum, and it is the starting place for moving beyond being a wanderer. No longer do you have to be someone who aspires to live your God-inspired dreams but cannot seem to move those dreams along.

In the previous chapter, I introduced blue-collar goal setting as the first of 10 Trailblazer's Rhythms to help move your dreams into reality. The next five rhythms I call the "foundational rhythms" because they concentrate on the importance of continual progress. These are: focus on the next small step, celebrate short-term wins, maintain momentum, adjust as clarity presents, and maintain a manageable pace.

If you are already planning ambitiously, it's time to start preparing persistently by incorporating these rhythms into your daily and weekly routines.

Trailblazer's Rhythm 2: Focus on the Next Small Step

I have found that most people abandon the climb toward their goal once the journey ahead looks too imposing or difficult. It is, therefore, important to break the journey down into small attainable steps. Stay focused on the next step and do not lose momentum. Start by breaking down your God-inspired dream into small steps that will move you incrementally toward your goal. Some of those steps will become evident as you ask the stop-start-keep questions of blue-collar goal setting, and then work weekly to accomplish the next small step. Do not worry about how you will accomplish step number 10, or even step 2 and 3. All that matters now is step number 1—the one that's right in front of you. As I said earlier, I rarely plan far out in the future. The future may look different after accomplishing step number one. I have discovered that *clarity comes with momentum.*

When I first got serious about being involved in the search for Noah's ark, I was almost forty years old, and I knew nothing about mountaineering. In fact, I had never even climbed a large mountain. The dream seemed unrealistic. My mind wanted to run five steps ahead to try and deal with the huge unknowns: *How would I ever get in contact with someone who was currently searching for the ark? And if I did get in contact with someone, why would they want me to be a part of their team? What value did I bring?*

Thinking beyond the very next step in the journey is a recipe for discouragement, fear, and eventually defeat.

Step number one in my search for Noah's ark was to gain information on the subject. As an entrepreneur, husband, and father of five, I had limited time to work on my dream of finding the ark. I did find time here and there to search the Internet or read a book. Through reading extensively on the subject, I learned all I could about the present day search. After a while, I came to understand who the legitimate players were. One week my only goal was deciding who the best person would be for me to make an initial contact with regarding the search. If I let my mind think about actually calling the person, I started getting fearful. I was afraid of how the conversation might go. *How would I answer the questions about my qualifications? What if they rejected me? Would my dream be over?*

Remember, clarity comes with momentum. Just put your energy each and every week into the very next small step.

 ### *Trailblazer's Rhythm 3: Celebrate Short-Term Wins*

I discovered the importance of this principle while running my business. As with many organizations, it often seemed that we were having more problems than positive results.

The leadership team has always gathered once a week for a planning meeting. Years ago the focus of those meetings had a tendency to gravitate toward problem areas. Now, I know that problem areas have to be dealt with; part of effective leadership is refusing to turn a blind eye to the challenges. But constantly dealing with challenges also drains energy. And on far too many occasions I was leaving those meetings worn out and discouraged. I knew we were doing good things as an organization, but it was hard to see those things through the fog of what seemed like continual challenges.

I decided to make a change. Each week I asked my leaders to bring to the meeting one positive result they were seeing in their area of responsibility. The positive didn't need to be a huge victory because huge victories were often hard to come by. We started off the meeting taking turns talking about the small victories we saw the previous week. We called those victories "short-term wins," and nicknamed them STWs. This practice totally changed the dynamics of the meeting. It was amazing to see the energy that was gained as we each took turns sharing our STW. Sometimes the entire meeting was spent sharing them. We found that focusing on the victories gave us the needed energy to respond more effectively to the challenges. The same is true when you pursue your God-inspired dream.

As you maintain momentum by focusing on your next small step, you are going to see one of two things happen. You will have either victorious moments or setbacks. But even these setbacks I like to call clarifying moments. And both are wins. When you accomplish a goal, you have experienced a STW. Take time to celebrate that victory with someone close to you. When you run up against an obstacle, you are experiencing a clarifying moment. Don't treat that as a defeat. What you have now is actually more clarity about which direction not to pursue. Or maybe what you have is more insight into what is required in order to continue along your dream journey. Clarifying moments are also STWs and should be treated as something to celebrate. When I encounter clarifying moments, I tell myself that I am more informed than I was before. Take time every week or so to review your STWs so you can experience the satisfaction of knowing you are creating momentum along the journey. Just remember, short-term wins equal progress. As long as you are making progress, you are living your dream.

 Trailblazer's Rhythm 4: Maintain Momentum

Nobody would say that moving your God-inspired dreams along is easy. But even harder than moving your dream along is getting your dream started in the first place. This is why it is so important that you maintain momentum once you have started making progress. In Jim Collin's excellent book *Good to Great* he talks about the flywheel principle. The following is an excerpt:

> Picture a huge, heavy flywheel. It's a massive metal disk mounted horizontally on an axle. It's about 100 feet in diameter, 10 feet thick, and it weighs about 25 tons. That flywheel is your company [or your God-inspired dream]. Your job is to get that flywheel to move as fast as possible, because momentum – mass times velocity – is what will generate superior results over time.
>
> Right now the flywheel is at a standstill. To get it moving, you make a tremendous effort. You push with all your might, and finally you get the flywheel to inch forward. After two or three days of sustained effort, you get the flywheel to complete one entire turn. You keep pushing, and the flywheel begins to move a bit faster. It takes a lot of work, but at last the flywheel makes a second rotation. You keep pushing steadily. It makes three turns, four turns, five, six. With each turn, it moves faster, and then – at some point, you can't say exactly when – you

break through. The momentum of the heavy wheel kicks in your favor. It spins faster and faster, with its own weight propelling it.

The lesson from the flywheel principle (in our context) is that it takes a lot of energy to get your God-inspired dream moving in the first place. So it's important that you not let your dream lose momentum. A push on the flywheel in this illustration is equivalent to taking the next small step along the dream journey. If you continue to take one step after another, you will build up momentum over time. Of course, everyone has periods of time when other pressing demands take priority. That's normal. But you shouldn't totally abandon all efforts toward your dream. If you do, you will lose valuable momentum. And that momentum takes significant energy to regain. Instead, make your next step really small. One idea might be to focus on gaining knowledge about your dream by researching online a little each week. Or maybe read a little bit each night on a subject that will better equip you for your dream. Give yourself the freedom to divert your energy toward more pressing demands as needed. Just make sure you keep tapping on the flywheel. The longer you go without a step, no matter the size, the harder it is to regain momentum. Keep moving forward.

 Trailblazer's Rhythm 5: Adjust as Clarity Presents

It's important to start living your dream today by giving yourself the freedom to adjust your dream as needed. Too often the temptation is to delay living your God-inspired dreams until you have all facets of the plan worked out ahead of time. This temptation keeps most people forever on the sidelines as they continually work to solve all the potential problems before they ever start. This same issue can tempt you to shape your dream into something you can logically get your arms around, all for the sake of feeling comfortable before getting started. In other words, you take the God-inspired dream that only God could accomplish and you reshape it into something that with hard work and determination you actually might be able to do under your own strength.

It's natural to take this approach. Textbook leadership says to create one-year, three-year, and even five-year plans and beyond. We have been taught that it's not wise to create plans that are unrealistic. Instead we're taught to create a logical roadmap that we can follow to accomplish our goals. If you do this, though, you will risk falling short of accomplishing the great things God has in store for you. In my own experience, my dream paths have not always followed a logical progression. One of my dreams has been to find and document the remains of Noah's ark. That in itself seems more fairytale than logical. Another dream I had was to write a book. I had no experience as a writer, but here I am at my desk writing a book. Both dreams are examples of how I surf life. I have navigated these dreams the same way I surf the woods. I start out in the general direction I think I need to go, and then I adjust accordingly. Remember, clarity will come with momentum.

As a wilderness explorer, before I head into an unfamiliar part of the forest I study a topography map to determine which areas look most interesting to explore. But as I head off into the woods on my adventure, I often notice that the area I had anticipated being beautiful or interesting is not as nice as I had expected. I often discover another area that is much more beautiful. The map provides some help. It gives me a starting point, but it is only once I'm on the ground inside the topography that I can actually see what the map represents. I enjoy the wilderness more fully by adjusting my bearings once I actually see what exists inside the woods. The same is true with pursuing God-inspired dreams: plan ambitiously, prepare persistently, but give yourself the freedom to adjust your dream accordingly as clarity presents.

Trailblazer's Rhythm 6: Maintain a Manageable Pace

The very first time I climbed above 14,000 feet is still vivid in my mind. It was Mt. Yale in Colorado. My friends and I got an early start, and I felt great. Only one friend had experience at high elevation. He kept alluding to how hard it was going to be. I paid very little attention. I was an experienced outdoorsman, or so I thought. *How could this be anything more than a challenging hike?* During the first mile the experienced friend kept telling me to slow down and pace myself. He said the climb would get far more difficult above 12,000 feet. He encouraged me to find a steady rhythm that I could maintain; otherwise, I might not make it to the top of the mountain. Being the stubborn guy that I am, another friend and I pushed way out ahead. I felt like I was in far better shape than the experienced friend who was giving us this advice. And after all, I was used to hiking plenty of miles through the Ozark Mountains of Arkansas. Judging by the first few hours, this climb was going to be no problem.

Hours later we finally broke above 12,000 feet. I was breathing much more rapidly and my legs began to weaken. By 13,000 feet I was exhausted. I could only go about fifty yards at a time before I would have to stop and rest. I could see the top of the mountain. It looked so close, but I was making very little progress at that point. I was too winded. It felt like I had concrete boots for shoes. Within an hour my experienced friend had caught up with us and passed us on the final ridgeline. I must confess that I didn't make it all the way to the top. I ran out of steam just short. I could see it, but I just couldn't make it.

It is as critical in life as it is in mountain climbing—if you are going to last on an ambitious journey, you need to maintain a manageable pace. Being successful at living your God-inspired dreams requires that you take a marathoner's approach. We all know that a marathoner runs much differently than a sprinter. He has to conserve his energy so he can last all 26 miles. It would be silly for a marathoner to approach a race by saying, "My strategy is going to be to run as fast as I can all the way to the finish line." That would be ignorant. Even the best marathon runners would not last for the entire race if they tried to run like a sprinter. Marathoners spread their energy out over the entire race.

You have to look at living your God-inspired dreams the way a marathoner looks at running; you have to pace yourself. Unless you are independently wealthy, or maybe retired, you probably have the demands of a job. You may be married and have children at home. All of those elements of your life require time and energy. If you have any extra time at all, you probably look for ways to relax rather then spend it on an ambitious dream that requires time, money, perseverance, and faith. Believe it or not, I can relate.

I was already exhausted with life when God started waking me up to the ambitious vision He had laid on my heart: a vision for helping men resist the pull toward complacency. I was raising five children, trying to be a good husband, struggling to run a business, and trying to be a leader at church. I was doing all of this while working to stay current with the mountain of bills. Carving out a piece of my day to start living an ambitious dream journey just seemed impossible. That was until my life coach encouraged me to pace myself by aligning as much of the current activities in my life as I could toward my larger vision. And then he showed me how I could focus weekly on taking one small step at a time toward this vision. With his help, I started living my dreams right then by helping the people that were already around me to resist complacency. I saw my interactions at work, church, and home as a training ground for the larger vision God had given me. I also started to align my leisure time with the activities that fueled my dreams. Instead of spending four hours on an activity like golf that had little benefit toward my dreams, I took the same time and spent it in the wilderness refining my skills as an outdoorsman.

Often when I go to bed, I unwind by reading for fifteen to twenty minutes. I started making sure that whatever I read during that time was better equipping me for my dream journey. At church, I stopped volunteering for things that did not align with my God-inspired dreams. I chose, instead, to impact my church in those areas where I could influence men. In short, I used what I call my *motivating impact zone* (the cause or people group that you desire to impact) as a guideline for where I gave my very limited time and money. Thinking about life this way helped me pace myself, and it gave me some boundaries by which to prioritize my efforts.

What are the boundaries by which you want to prioritize your time, efforts, and money? Make sure those boundaries focus your life on your unique God-inspired dreams. After you have those boundaries established, take a closer look at how you can start making an impact with your life right away at work, at home, in your neighborhood, and at church. Steer away from activities and efforts that don't align with your larger vision. After a few weeks and months, your life will be in greater harmony with your larger vision. You won't be so worn out. Your days will be more energizing, and your efforts will prove more satisfying. You'll be in a much better position to pace yourself for the marathon of life.

Caffeinated Questions

1. What short-term win (STW) did you experience recently?

2. What next step forward will you take this week in relationship to your dreams?

3. Based on your motivating impact zone, what boundaries should you use to focus your time, efforts, and money?

PERSEVERE COURAGEOUSLY

CHAPTER FIVE

Persevere Courageously

Keep away from those who try to belittle your ambitions. Small people always do that, but the really great make you believe that you too can become great.

—Mark Twain

The rest of the expedition team finally joined us on the eastern plateau of Mount Ararat. It had been almost a week since we left them behind and proceeded to the ice cap. After our brush with death a couple of days earlier, I was taking no chances. From now on, my GPS and compass were going with me everywhere on this crazy mountain. At last we had everything we needed to complete the dig—chainsaws for cutting ice blocks, slam bars for breaking up the ice, and more shovels for clearing debris; and finally, we had more people to complete the back-breaking work.

On the first day with a full team, the weather was nice and the dig progressed rapidly. We estimated four or five days of excavating to get down to the structure. We assumed that the structure was full of ice, so there would likely be no way to climb inside and look around. That being the case, our primary goal was to retrieve wood from the structure that we could take for radiocarbon dating.

On day two, about noon, the weather began turning ugly again. We retreated to our tents for what we hoped would be a couple hours of rest while the storm blew over. But those couple of hours dragged into three of the longest days of my life.

It's really hard to understand the rigors of mountaineering until you have experienced it for yourself. When most people think about climbing mountains, they picture the arduous climbs carrying heavy backpacks in thin, cold air. That is a difficult part of mountaineering, but I have found tent life to be even more challenging. Imagine lying on your back on a thin pad huddled in your sleeping bag for days at a time, hoping for a break in the weather. When you do choose to get out of your sleeping bag, you cannot stand up, because there's not enough headroom in the tent. Therefore, you sit cross-legged for a while. The cramped, gloomy confines of the tent prove depressing. A few minutes out of the bag and your body gets cold, so back in the sleeping bag you go. Then there are those times when you have to use the bathroom. You're lucky if you are a guy, and all you have to do is pee. In that case, you keep a bottle by your sleeping bag and relieve yourself into the bottle, making sure to keep a tight lid on the bottle when you are finished. It's unfortunate for you if you have to drop your drawers for a bowel movement. You try and put it off as long as you can. Finally, you get your boots on, leave the tent, and endure the terrible weather conditions while squatting in the snow. After you are through, you finish it off with an alpine wipe. Basically, that is using a snowball instead of toilet paper. Mountaineering is punishing on all levels.

During the second night in the tents, the wind got exceptionally strong. Kevin and I were sleeping in an extremely tough NorthFace® four-season alpine tent. These tents are made for tough mountaineering conditions, but nonetheless our tent was taking a beating and we were concerned that it might not hold up. We also had reason to fear for some of the other members on the team. A few of the guys had brought along three-season tents to save some weight, but those tents aren't made for high-altitude mountaineering where you can experience ferocious winds. I was awakened several times during the night as the wind was pushing the south side of our tent down on my face. I tried to sleep holding the tent wall up off my body with my right arm. I could feel the snow and hail on my arm through the two thin layers of nylon tent that protected us. Finally with one punishing burst of wind, the tent collapsed across our bodies. We instantly got to our knees and held the tent up across our arms. Fortunately for us, only one tent pole had broken in half from the wind, and we were able to rig up a quick fix from inside the tent. If this wind was punishing our tent so violently, things had to be worse for many of the other team members.

A few hours later we heard one of the Kurdish porters frantically screaming some words we couldn't understand. It turned out that two of our team members' tents had been completely ripped apart from the punishing winds. One took refuge in another's tent. The other man, Richard Bright, lay seemingly lifeless in the snow, the walls of his tent having been completely torn away. No one was sure how long he had been lying there exposed to the elements. Given the buildup of snow around his sleeping bag, it had been quite some time. Richard was our expedition leader, and he was the glue that held our team together. He was a tireless searcher for the ark, having made over twenty-five trips to Mount Ararat. Over those decades, he had carefully cultivated relationships with the Kurdish and the Turkish people that live around the mountain. It was because of those relationships that we had greater access to the mountain than all others who searched for the ark. Richard treated the Kurdish and Turkish people with great respect, and they loved him like a family member. Kevin and one of the Kurdish men carefully moved him out of the storm and into another man's tent. He wasn't very responsive, and they worked to warm him. He was in his sixties, and I wondered if he would fully recover from this near hypothermic incident.

The next day about 10:00 a.m. the weather finally broke, and the sun came bursting through the clouds. We emerged from our tents to survey the damage. It was disheartening to say the least. Nearly everyone's tent had experienced some damage. Two were completely ruined. The good news was Richard was feeling pretty good considering the rough night he had just experienced. The two Kurdish porters, whose job it was to cook, abandoned us early that morning. We had no food, very little fuel, and unreliable shelter. We had to retreat back down the mountain and reevaluate our next step. As we walked off the eastern plateau that day, we passed by our dig location. It was completely filled back in with snow. Three hard days of digging left us with nothing. Thoughts ran through my mind about whether this was really worth the effort. *Maybe God didn't want us looking for the ark. If God was in this search, why were we experiencing such harsh weather conditions? After all, doesn't God control the weather? Who are we to try and fight God's will?* As we made our way back down the mountain, I wrestled with thoughts of quitting. Maybe this was all just a sign for me to stop pursuing this dream and retreat to the safe zone.

After several hours of careful descent, we were back down to the safety of the 14,000-foot camp. Hungry and tired, we all gathered in the meal tent and stuffed ourselves with whatever calories we could find. One of the Kurdish men came in and handed a cell phone to Richard. We had been out of communication with the leader of our Kurdish team since we had left the safety of the 14,000-foot camp the week before. I could see by the expression on Richard's face that he was receiving some troubling news. The year before we had received eyewitness reports that a portion of the ark was buried near the foot of the Parrot Glacier on another side of the mountain at lower elevation. Months earlier we had rented some heavy equipment and hired some local men to begin pushing a road into this particular area of the mountain. Once the locals reached the location they were to begin excavating the site. The plan was to join this team after we had finished our work higher up on the eastern plateau. Richard hung up the phone with a look of frustration across his face. Nothing could prepare us for the words we were about to hear: "The PKK has captured the team working at the lower sight, burned all of our equipment, and are holding the men hostage." Things just went from bad to worse. *How could we fight against this kind of adversity?* I hung my head and felt the fear building up in me. *Were we going to be captured next?* That afternoon we made camp and prepared for one last night on the mountain. As I lay there, I began folding up this ambitious dream, as if to put it away in an old storage shed, never to be experienced again. I thought surely this dream was now dead.

If you plan to live ambitiously, know that you will encounter the kind of challenges that will test the very foundation of your will. I have found considerable truth in the saying, "Good things don't come easy." But that does not mean good things are impossible. It just means you'd better be prepared to hang tough and cling tight to the third dreamer's principle.

Dreamer's Principle 3: Persevere Courageously

> When troubles come your way, consider it an opportunity
> for great joy. For you know that when your faith is tested,
> your endurance has a chance to grow. So let it grow, for
> when your endurance is fully developed, you will be
> perfect and complete, needing nothing.
>
> —James 1:2–4 (NLT)

Effective dreamers will inevitably encounter difficulties as they pursue their ambitious goals. Pushing through those difficulties requires character and fortitude. The Bible tells us in James 1:2–4 that character comes through perseverance. The more you persevere, the more character you will have to help you live your God-inspired dreams successfully. It's character that God uses to fuel and stabilize your success. You won't be able to shortcut the process. In fact, James 1:2 tells us to embrace troubles with joy. Instead of getting upset when difficulties happen, look for the endurance to welcome those difficulties as necessary character builders. A successful dream journey is going to be riddled with situations that will require faith and perseverance. Those situations are never easy, but they can be managed successfully; ultimately, they're even good for us. First and foremost, you have to establish deep roots in the promises of Scripture in order to focus your mind on truth when facing difficulty. I have memorized Philippians 4:4–8 (NLT), because it gives excellent guidance on how to properly position your mind when facing challenges.

> Always be full of joy in the Lord. I say it again—rejoice!
> Let everyone see that you are considerate in all you do.
> Remember, the Lord is coming soon. Don't worry about
> anything; instead, pray about everything. Tell God what

you need, and thank him for all he has done. Then you will experience God's peace, which exceeds anything we can understand. His peace will guard your hearts and minds as you live in Christ Jesus.

My favorite translation of verse 8 (the HCSB) reads:

Whatever is true, whatever is honorable, whatever is just, whatever is pure, whatever is lovely, whatever is commendable—if there is any moral excellence and if there is any praise—dwell on these things.

Verse 8 reminds me not to sit around crippled by fear and worrying about all the what-if scenarios. In difficult situations, we are told to keep a positive outlook, by dwelling on positive things—truth, not what-ifs. And as we see in the previous verses, we can gain protection against what-if thinking by giving God our concerns in prayer and by thanking Him for how He has been faithful in the past.

If you establish deep roots in the truths found in Scripture, you will be prepared mentally to persevere courageously, but you won't sidestep the places in the journey that require faith and courage. That is where the next two trailblazer's rhythms can be helpful: seize the moments, and don't journey alone. These I call the courageous rhythms.

 ### Trailblazer's Rhythm 7: Seize the Moments

As you walk along your dream journey, focusing on the next small step and working hard to persevere, occasionally an ambitious opportunity will present itself. All your previous small steps will lead you to this moment. Taking another small step will seem out of order. It is a bold step that is needed, a bold step that takes courage. These are critical moments that you must seize. I have found these to be God ordained, and they tend to require faith in order to accomplish them. It's the small steps that set the pace for moving your dream along effectively. But it's the bold steps that open the curtain to new vistas for accelerated progress. Don't try to execute around them. Seize them!

Several years ago I had started a small line of Christian apparel called CrossEyed Wear. We had placed the line in Christian bookstores across the country and were seeing limited success. One night my business partner, Scott, was watching ESPN. The starting quarterback for the St. Louis Rams, Kurt Warner, was being interviewed. Scott noticed that Kurt Warner was wearing a CrossEyed t-shirt during the interview. When he came to work the next day, he told me about it. I decided to take the small step of finding out the mailing address of the St. Louis Rams field house. After a quick search online, I had the address. Then came a bold-step moment. I needed to get in contact with Kurt Warner. What better way to help promote my Christian line of apparel than to have Kurt Warner wearing it?

I grabbed a handful of CrossEyed t-shirts and sent them in an overnight package to the address I had found. I enclosed a letter thanking Kurt for wearing our product and I gave him my contact information. This was the next logical step in pursuit of my goal, and to me it also felt like a bold step. The next day I was helping in the warehouse when I was paged over the intercom: "Holt, Kurt Warner is on line one." I wondered if this was a joke. Fear gripped me as I readied myself to pick up the phone. What does a guy who runs a t-shirt business say to a star quarterback of the NFL? I picked up the phone, and it actually was Kurt Warner on the other end of the line. We had a great conversation in which he happily agreed to help me promote CrossEyed Wear. It was the beginning of a fun association that I will never forget.

If you are truly walking the ambitious path God has for you, you won't have to try and invent these moments. God will present them in His timing if you persevere. Just stay committed to focusing on the next small step in order to maintain momentum. Pray for God to help you see clearly the bold steps as He presents them. And pray for the courage to walk boldly into those moments.

 ### *Trailblazer's Rhythm 8: Don't Journey Alone*

Several years ago I heard the story about a wild cave with an interesting history near my property in the Ozarks. A local man told me that Indians often frequented the cave. When he was a boy, his father told him stories about going deep in the cave. Inside it was a room filled with Indian artifacts. His father told him that sometime in his lifetime the entrance to this room must have collapsed, because he had not been able to find the room when he returned to it as an adult. It sounded like the perfect adventure for me, so after getting directions to its location, a friend and I set off to explore.

After about an hour of heavy bushwhacking, we found the cave entrance hidden beneath a bluff. Equipped with headlamps, kneepads, and helmets, we dropped off into the cave. Once inside, we stayed together as we squirmed for an hour or so through the passages. Time was running short. We hadn't found the secret room we were looking for, so we started making our way out. Near the exit we found two small tunnels that we hadn't seen on our way in. Knowing that we had limited time, he took one tunnel, and I took the other. These passages were very tight; as I squirmed through the passage on my belly, I began to worry that I might get stuck. I could see the passage went another ten yards or so and appeared to open up to a larger room beyond. As I debated about moving forward, I became gripped with fear. I was in a tight space by myself, and I feared if I kept inching forward I might not be able to get out. I was wishing my friend were with me just in case I got stuck and needed his help. Little did I know he was fighting the same battle with fear in the other tunnel. Overwhelmed by anxiety, we both backed out of our respective tunnels that day and left the cave never knowing if we were just a short distance away from the treasure.

I often look back on that adventure with regret. Was I only ten yards from a room full of Indian history? But I now use that regret as a reminder to walk life's difficult moments in partnership with others. Courage comes in connection with those around us. I have learned in my business to surround myself with good leaders and lean on them often. One of the things we practice in our meetings at Ink is transparency about our fears as leaders. It's amazing how much courage is gained when I express my fears to others I can trust. The burdens get distributed across the shoulders of the team rather than pressing down on mine alone, and I realize that I have others in the fight with me. If I am facing a challenging conversation with a client or a team member, I tell my business partner about my fears. Often he offers to take a piece of the challenge on himself or he gives me an encouraging perspective on how to handle the difficulty. After we talk, I'm emboldened to walk forward into the challenge. Without those conversations, I often shrink back and procrastinate or even wither away from facing it altogether.

The same holds true as I walk my God-inspired dreams. To help me be more successful, I have surrounded myself with a few men who have similar visions. We join arms to help each other achieve our respective goals. We often get together to celebrate our short-term wins and talk through our corresponding next small steps. If one of us is encountering an obstacle or having trouble persevering, we express our fears, gain courage, and find our way forward.

Do not find yourself alone and overwhelmed in the fog of life. Reach out and walk in step with those who have similar beliefs and values. I have found these like-minded individuals by taking a risk and opening up my dream door to those around me. Having the courage to step forward and share my dreams has given them the opportunity to share theirs as well.

Occasionally, God will place you on a path with someone who has visions and values that complement yours. You should invite that person a little deeper into your life. Some will become friends that you decide to do life with regularly, and others will prove to be only acquaintances. Go deep with the friends and limit your time with the acquaintances. I have a handful of very close friends that I spend time with face-to-face regularly. I go to those people to get advice. Sometimes we ask each other to share in the load. I cannot meet regularly with acquaintances and still maintain a manageable pace. I look at my less frequent encounters with acquaintances as opportunities for God to allow me to use the gift He has given me as an igniter; a person who provides spark to people's passion. Those meetings are still a blessing in that they encourage the individual, I hope; and they encourage and energize me, as well, because I get a chance to interact in line with the way God designed me.

Your important role as a dream-door opener

When one of my daughters was younger, she enjoyed participating in team sports. She was a very competitive young lady, and team sports were a healthy outlet for that competitive nature. She tried basketball first, then moved on to softball. She didn't have the kind of success she had hoped for in either of those sports, so she decided to give soccer a try. One night, in her second year of soccer at age sixteen, I picked her up at school after she had returned from an away game. She got off the bus and climbed inside the truck rather frustrated—something had obviously gone wrong. We sat there in silence for a few minutes until I broke the tension with that question a dad often fears to ask, "Is everything okay?" That's when the tears started.

"Dad, I wasn't good at basketball. I wasn't good at softball. And I'm not good at soccer either. I try so hard, and it doesn't seem to matter. I just want to give up."

I wasn't sure what to say. Right before my eyes, I was watching her dream door close. This was a perfect example of what happens often in our lives that causes us to shut down and seek refuge in the safe zone. I needed to move in with a rescue plan. The rest of the drive home I reassured her of the strengths God had given her, and how in time He would use those strengths for powerful impact if she would put them to use for His glory. I was trying to focus her attention on her strengths and away from her weaknesses. Once I had her attention on her strengths, she began to open up again about her dreams.

If you don't work hard to help someone keep their dream door wide open, they will close it all together. When that happens, they will stop thinking ambitiously in all aspects of their lives, even in areas where they have natural strengths. That's the beginning of a disappointing life. As a parent or a friend, you must find a careful balance in steering people toward their strengths while giving them a chance to explore their weaknesses. I have found both to be important.

I wonder what kind of impact the church could have if we all worked harder at opening wide one another's dream doors. I have shared my dreams with many a pastor who unknowingly poured cold water all over it. Those same pastors wonder why they stare across the congregation at many people that seem uninspired and unmotivated. I have had men in Christian ministry take my God-inspired dreams and somehow try to fit them into their programs and ideas about how ministry should work in relationship to their own personal goals. They may have been well-intentioned, but they were, in effect, closing my dream door.

There's nothing wrong with helping someone bring clarity from confusion. In fact, that's what you should do, especially if a significant life change is involved. You are doing that person a favor if you help him take intelligent steps toward ambitious dreams. For example, I would never encourage anyone to leave his job and go to Africa to be a missionary based on a feeling he got from a recent missions trip. But it would be appropriate to sit down with that person and clarify his calling against the way God uniquely designed him. Above all, I would strive to keep his dream door open by steering him toward ambitious goals that do make sense based on his calling (a subject I will write about later).

In my opinion, dream door opening may be one of the most important roles of the local church. In reality, the church often performs terribly in this role. It's time for a change and it can start with you. There is an incredible power within you to help shape another person's life for the better. All you have to do is use the magic words. When someone has the courage to share their dreams with you try saying, "Wow! That sounds interesting. Tell me more about it."

Lonely Warrior

I stand in the battle. Where are my weapons?
I run to fight. Where is my sword?
I look for defense. Where is my armor?
My wounds give me pain. Where is my shield?
I look for protection. Where are my allies?
I turn to flee. Where is my camp?

I look up to You. Your face filled with anguish.
As tears fill Your eyes, my confidence grows.

The ground starts to shake as You saddle Your horses.
Thunder comes down as You scream out commands.
You rush down from heaven and run to my rescue.

Where are my enemies now?

You reach out Your arm. You place it around me.
I lean on Your shoulder. I start to cry.
You survey my wounds and tenderly heal them.
You open my mind and help me see why.

Why did You place me in battle? I had no sword by my side.
No shield for protection. No chariot to ride.
I'm willing to fight but give me some weapons.
And if I am hurt, give me some place to hide.

Son, there is a purpose for every wound that you felt.
Though it was painful, I had hearts to melt.
Look for your enemies. Where did they go?
Survey the field. Where is your foe?

Looking up from His shoulder, I glance all around.
I see not my enemies, but allies I've found.

These now are your allies but enemies they were.
Because of your anguish, their hearts I could stir.
I placed you in weakness to demonstrate power.
Because you were faithful, rewards I will shower.

Caffeinated Questions

1. What are the areas of your life where you feel like quitting? Why?

2. Who are the people that have helped push you through quitting points?

3. Are you currently sharing you burdens with a friend? Why or why not?

CHAPTER SIX

Overload

We don't drift in good directions. We discipline and prioritize
ourselves there.

—Andy Stanley

There's a beautiful park near my home in Little Rock called Pinnacle
Mountain State Park. Inside that park is a wonderful little mountain
called Pinnacle that has approximately 800 feet of elevation gain
from trailhead to summit. The trails up, down, and around Pinnacle
Mountain are etched in my brain. I know every inch of them. I would
venture to say that very few people know those trails as well as I do.
I have spent countless hours on that mountain training as a climber;

transforming myself physically and mentally. I have spent so much time training on Pinnacle Mountain that when I pull up in my Jeep for an afternoon workout; it feels like I'm coming home to a friend.

I was forty when I finally decided to put feet to my desire to pursue the final resting place of Noah's ark. I was overweight, out of shape, and I knew nothing about climbing mountains. To bring value to an ark search expedition, I was going to have to become somewhat of a mountaineer. I would not only have to be trained in the skills of climbing, but even more importantly I would have to get myself in shape for the challenges of climbing. Seventeen years of the stress that comes with entrepreneurship had taken a toll on my body. I am a small guy at five foot eight, but I weighed nearly 200 pounds. That was far too much weight on my frame for the riggers of the mountains. I was strong, but out of shape. I can remember a friend of mine looking at me one day and telling me that I needed to lose some weight if I was serious about climbing. It was just the kick in the butt that I needed. I began transforming myself into climbing condition with a process I call overload.

Trailblazer's Rhythm 9: Overload!

Overload has changed the way I approach challenges. I use this rhythm across all facets of my life. I use it to train for tough climbs up big mountains carrying heavy backpacks. I use it to shed a few pounds or carve a couple of inches off my waist from time to time. I use it to grow my business. I use it to improve my financial situation. I use it to memorize scripture.

Overload is the process of slowly and consistently elevating the stress level of an activity toward whatever goal you have in mind. It is the idea of taking a very slow, but increasingly intense, approach toward the results you want. I discovered this principle by spending many hours training my body with physical exercise and watching how it reacts to the strain.

I have always been drawn to activities where I can push my body to its limits. After a day of meetings, client visits, and working in front of the computer, I am usually looking for a way to give my body a good workout. Sometimes I hit the trails around Arkansas to exert some energy. Other times a visit to the weight room fills the need, as it has for much of my life. In order to reach my goals for size, strength, and endurance, I have tried all kinds of training programs over the years.

Some years ago I read an article in a fitness magazine. The author wrote about the importance of continually putting your muscles under ever-increasing stress in order to get progressive results. For example, if you want to increase the size of your chest, you will likely want to make the bench press a part of your workout routine. If one week you bench press 135 pounds 8 times, the next week you would need to try 140 pounds 8 times, or you may choose 135 pounds 9 times. Either way, you would be practicing progressive overload. Then the next week you would need to go up in intensity again, and so on every week thereafter. I have found the results are amazing. Every week you see another short-term win when you use progressive overload.

Let me give you a present day example of how I am using overload to help me be successful on my dream journey. When I plan to go to Mount Ararat, I start training months before I leave. I have to have my body prepared to spend three weeks at an elevation of nearly 17,000 feet above sea level. I will also need to be prepared to carry 45–50 pounds on my back, in thin air, for the last 3,500 feet of elevation. As I am writing this, I plan to leave for Mount Ararat on August 5. That is five months away. I would not be sufficiently ready to be successful on Mount Ararat if I were leaving today. To get myself prepared, I use progressive overload.

I start by giving myself plenty of time to make slow, steady progress toward my goal. I am fortunate that my friend, Pinnacle Mountain, is near my home where I can train for my climbs. Three times this week I will carry 15 pounds up and down the mountain twice for the equivalent of 1,600 feet of elevation gain. Over the next five months, I will slowly increase the intensity on my body until I feel comfortable carrying 45–50 pounds over 3,500 feet of elevation gain. Is it possible to get ready faster? Yes. But a quicker approach also puts me at greater risk for failure from injury and/or burnout. That only leads to discouragement that could put me on the fast track to the safe zone. When I get ready to accomplish any significant goal, I always try to give myself plenty of time to take a slow and increasingly intense approach toward it. By giving myself plenty of time, I am assured a greater chance of success.

Maybe your body is no longer strong and healthy, and you believe it may be holding you back from walking the dream journey God has for you. It's time to overload! Don't try crazy get-slim-quick approaches that are typically doomed for failure. Take a slow and increasingly intense approach. Try taking six months to very slowly lower your calorie count, while at the same time steadily increasing the length and intensity of your aerobic activity. Maybe you want to quit smoking. Overload! Take a slow and steady approach by reducing the amount you smoke a little more each week. It might be best to take six to nine months to achieve this goal. It could be that you want to start reading your Bible more consistently. Start with five minutes a day and overload.

You may be obsessing over an issue, and you need to find a way to break the grip that issue has on your life. Maybe the habit that once was a good thing has now turned out to be an unhealthy obsession, like exercising or keeping your house clean. Slowly get those routines back in their proper boundaries with overload.

The important thing is to avoid failure by, in effect, not shocking your mind, body, and emotions with the change. If you start off with insignificant changes to your routine, and then continue toward your goal with slow progress, your mind and body adjust with better success. Our bodies and minds are designed to protect against sudden changes. If you do not believe me, go on a crash diet, and your body will react by trying to store fat, lower your energy level, and increase your appetite. Eventually you will likely go back to the same unhealthy eating habits you had before the diet. Instead, try eating 50 calories less on day one and your body won't even notice.

Perhaps you seldom take time to read your Bible, but you feel the need to start. That's a great idea, but setting a goal of thirty minutes a day in the first week is likely a recipe for failure. If you start off that strong, three weeks later you will likely be hit-or-miss on reading your Bible at all. Your mind cannot adjust easily to that much change to its routine. Start with five minutes of reading, and your mind will welcome the difference.

You may want to write a book, but the only time you have to write is during the evening when you like to relax and watch television. Overload! Very slowly wean yourself from the television and toward your writing. Before you know it, you will have substituted a bit more productivity for a bit less leisure.

I practice this principle at work, as I lead my company through changes and challenges. When I make significant changes at Ink, I try to incorporate them gradually. I picture Ink more like a ship than a speedboat. A ship turns very slowly. So much so that the passengers on the ship cannot even feel the change in direction. Make a quick turn on a speedboat, and if you are not careful, you will throw someone overboard. And remember, we want *overload*, not *overboard*!

Several years ago I took a risk and decided that there was a need to make a significant change in the direction my company was headed. That change involved adding a new division that I believed would open the door to a new type of client and potentially increase profits. We made slow, steady progress toward that goal in such a way that the current clients never felt the change, and our employees were able to comfortably adjust. But five years into the adjustments, we were not seeing the bottom-line results we needed to see, so we are now in the third year of steering the ship back toward the core competencies on which I founded the company. Leading in this manner conveys stability to your clients and employees and gives you a greater opportunity for success. It is okay to take risks and make changes even though some of those changes will prove to be failures. Just admit the failure and then make slow and steady progress back to better waters. If you use speedboat leadership, you risk losing good people. And before long your boat may sink. But if you want to make positive changes successfully, start off slowly then . . . overload.

Caffeinated Questions

1. What areas or habits in your life are you unhappy with?

2. How can you gain traction by using overload?

Chris Sims, me, and my business partner, Scott Masters, climbing Mount Yale. I was out of shape and unprepared for my first climb up a big mountain.

Training at Pinnacle Mountain State Park, Arkansas.

One of many beautiful waterfalls I discovered in the Leatherwood
Wilderness of Arkansas.

Coaching guys on a *Surf the Woods* retreat.

Speaking at a *Surf the Woods* men's retreat.

Mount Ararat, Turkey stands at 16,854 ft.

Kurdish porters climbing Mount Ararat with supplies.

Climbing to the summit of Mount Ararat.

Expedition camp on Mount Ararat.

Pulling the Ground Penetrating Radar instrument.

Our meal tent at high camp on Mount Ararat after wind damage.

Enjoying coffee with two of my Kurdish climbing friends.

Copperhead Cave near Jasper, Arkansas.

Ink Custom Tees.

Screenprinting t-shirts at Ink Custom Tees.

Mary, Chase, Courtney, Brady and Heather Condren.

ACCELERATE TOWARD FEAR

CHAPTER SEVEN

Prioritize Paradoxically

*Our schedules get packed with the mundane and the ordinary,
and we become irritated with God when He interrupts us with
the miraculous and extraordinary.*

—Erwin McManus

We made our way back down Mount Ararat to the small city of
Dogubayazit where we spent several days evaluating our next move.
Our Kurdish partners were working to secure the release of the men
being held hostage. The word from our Kurdish negotiator was the
PKK was upset that we had pushed a road up into the mountain.
They felt the road allowed the Turkish military better access to their

strongholds, and they did not want us to continue. After a few days, the PKK released all but a few of the men; most of the remaining hostages were Kurdish. Interestingly enough, the PKK felt that the discovery of Noah's ark on Mount Ararat would be a good thing for the Kurdish people, but in their minds the timing was not right. They gave us no clear reason as to why it was bad timing. We speculated that it had something to do with how it might affect their escalating skirmishes with the Turkish military.

As negotiations continued, a few of the American members of our team left for home. Our dig permit was running out, and the Kurdish men were not willing to risk staying on top of Mount Ararat without a secure structure. Those of us that remained decided that the only way to continue the dig on the eastern plateau was to assemble a secure structure next to the dig site; something we could prefabricate in town at the base of the mountain, and then reassemble on the plateau. The plan still presented plenty of challenges, but we felt it was worth a try. It would be used as a safe house against the violent weather and would be a much better place to eat together and keep warm. We contracted with a local Kurdish builder who prefabricated a 10-foot square structure using steel tubing and corrugated plastic sheeting. The plan was to disassemble it, and then have horses carry it up the mountain in pieces to the 14,000-foot camp. After that point, it would have to be carried the rest of the way on the backs of the Kurdish porters. Once at the dig site, we would reassemble the building and begin the dig all over again.

We decided that two other American team members and I would lead this effort. Once we had everything in place and were digging again, the rest of the team would join us. I can remember the day we started back up the mountain. I questioned whether I had the strength to endure another two weeks on Ararat. Climbing a 17,000-foot mountain is punishing to your body, and my body was still feeling the effects from my first time up and down. I had lost considerable weight, and my toes were suffering from boot bang, an extremely painful toe injury sustained while descending. After a couple of days climbing, we got back up to the 14,000-foot camp. Conspicuously absent were the pieces of structure I was to accompany to the top. It had taken longer than expected to assemble the horse team that was to transport the structure.

Over the next two days the weather deteriorated, and my two remaining American partners had enough. They were tired of waiting for the structure to arrive. Patience was wearing thin between the Kurdish team members and my fellow American climbers. They decided to return to Dogubayazit, and I would have to direct the effort on my own.

I remember watching my partners as they began their descent. It was a lonely feeling. I crawled into my tent and tried to sleep away my anxiousness. What was I doing all alone in this strange and dangerous place with no one around that could speak my language? I questioned my sanity as I recalled all the voices of my own dream-door slammers who had laughed at the idea of my chasing this dream in the first place.

The following day the pieces of the structure arrived, and the Kurdish porters talked about their plans to get the cargo up the mountain. They looked at the pieces in disbelief. I could see that they were not happy with the weight and size of the objects they were expected to carry. The initial plan was for the Kurdish men to carry the pieces of the structure up over several days while I waited at the 14,000-foot camp. Once all the pieces were at the top, then I would accompany the last load and begin reassembling. After that first day of climbing, the men came back down talking about the impossibility of the task. They said they could not find the dig location, and the money they were making was not worth the effort they were being asked to endure.

I could see that the plan was falling apart. I prayed for direction. I asked myself, *How badly do I really want this dream?* Tired and weary as I was, I knew that I had to find the strength to rally this group of men that I could hardly even communicate with. The next morning I awoke at 3:00 and went to the meal tent where the climbers typically gathered before the ascent. If this was going to get done, I decided I would have to lead by example. I would carry the structure up over the next several days alongside the Kurdish men, that is, if anybody showed up that morning for the climb. It was not what I wanted to do, but I knew I had to do it. I waited in the darkness as one man finally arrived. I could tell he was surprised to see me there. He went and awoke the others. By 4:00, we were all climbing together.

For five days in a row we awoke at 3:00, strapped awkward sheets of plastic, tube steel, and supplies to our backs, and made the grueling five-hour climb to the dig site. Once we reached the dig site we unloaded our cargo and made the two- to three-hour descent back to camp. This broke down all barriers between us as we struggled shoulder to shoulder, one American man and a bunch of Kurdish men. It was the toughest physical challenge I have ever endured. It took perseverance to a whole new level for me. On the fifth day another American team member joined us for the final ascent. That day we unloaded the last of the structure and began the reassembly. Three days later after digging had resumed, I headed back down the mountain to catch my flight back to the States. Six weeks after I arrived in Turkey, my part of the 2009 ark search was over.

Ambition and preparation are not worth much if you don't know which direction to head when you enter the persevering leg of your dream journey. Everyone needs a helpful trail map; otherwise, you run the risk of heading away from the rewarding life and toward the safe zone. You have to have direction indicators to help you stay on path toward your dream. In the mountains, we look for piles of rock called cairns. In the woods, we look for trail markers on trees. When you surf life, it's important that you do two things to gain direction and stay on track: prioritize paradoxically and accelerate toward fear.

Trailblazer's Rhythm 10: Prioritize Paradoxically

To prioritize paradoxically means that I prioritize my days and weeks opposite of the way I would normally prioritize. Going up and down Mount Ararat five days in a row while carrying heavy baggage was the opposite of what I wanted to do, but it had positive results for me as a leader. A paradox is like that. It is a surprising result that is often the opposite of what I expect. Most of us start off adulthood with high hopes for success in life, but before we know it, life has control of us rather than the other way around. We don't feel satisfied with where we are. What's happened, often subconsciously, is we have made a preponderance of choices toward what comes naturally and what comes easily. Then at some point, we wake up to the realization that we're not living the inspired life we had in mind. Living by prioritizing what comes naturally proves to be a highway to the safe zone. If I am going to make progress living the abundant life found in pursuit of my God-inspired dream, it's not going to come by doing what comes naturally. What comes naturally is laziness, passivity, whatever feels good at the moment, or giving attention to what just interrupted me.

As Steven Covey illustrates in his book *Seven Habits of Highly Effective People*, we should prioritize quadrant 2 activities (see diagram on next page). It is in these "Not urgent" and yet still "Important" activities where you will best progress toward your God-inspired dream. And where do you get the time for quadrant 2 activities? By carving it away from quadrants 3 and 4.

I try to prioritize these activities each day by asking the simple question, "What do I not want to do today that I know I really ought to do?" Whatever those one or two things are for the day, I attempt to move them to the top of my list. This is what it means to prioritize paradoxically. Often times those things are fears that I have to walk into. It might be a difficult phone call I need to make, having a hard conversation with a co-worker, finding the courage to pray with a family member over a troubling issue, or simply asking another person for help.

One of the things I love to do is eat breakfast while reading the newspaper. But oftentimes breakfast is the best time for one-on-one meetings with people that seek me out for encouragement. Naturally, I would prefer having breakfast by myself. However, if I prioritize paradoxically, I make the one-on-one breakfast a priority, and I am rewarded with another opportunity to use my gift igniting people's passions while they in turn bless me in the process. What I find over and over again as I try to live by this principle and teach it to those I coach is that I have so much more energy for life when I embrace the paradox. If I get off the couch and get to the gym, I end up with more energy, not less. If I walk into a troublesome relationship rather than avoid it, I end up with more energy, not less. If I call that potential large prospect and try to get an appointment, whether I get it or not, I end up with more energy after making the attempt. If I sit down with a friend and tell them I am sorry for hurting him, I gain energy from the effort.

As I write this book, I am reminded again of the importance of prioritizing paradoxically. I have felt drawn to write this book for a few years now, but it seemed silly on the surface, just like most dreams do. I discussed the idea with a few people. Most just brushed the idea away. Interestingly, though, that reaction has always been one of the indicators of whether or not I'm dreaming big enough to be in line with God's plans. If people seem to wholeheartedly come alongside my ideas as doable, I go back to the drawing board and try to think bigger. To me, even writing a book seemed almost like a fairytale because I'm not a trained writer. Who cares about what I have to say? I have few credentials that would draw people to embrace my teaching. Remember, my day job is running a custom t-shirt business. "Where would you even find time to write a book?" people asked.

My business partner and good friend, Scott, came alongside my idea and encouraged me to take the time to pursue this dream. Who better to encourage the effort than someone who is living one dream with me already? Based on the support of Scott and my family and friends, I worked my way through the process of writing this book by applying the principles set forth previously in the earlier chapters and prioritizing paradoxically. Perhaps I could have found more interesting things to do than sit in front of my laptop. I know I could have found more enjoyable things to do than type; I don't even know how to type! I hammered out the entire manuscript with two fingers. But I told myself that I would accomplish this because I felt called to write it. So each day I carved out a little time to write, and when I shut the computer off for the day, I felt energized by the effort. I knew that whether or not the book ever got published, I'd be a better person for pursuing the dream.

When you prioritize paradoxically in this fashion, you can lay your head on your pillow each night and know you are giving it your best effort. Come what may, you are moving away from the safe zone and toward the rewarding life.

Caffeinated Questions

1. What do you not want to do today (this week) that you know you really ought to do?

2. When will you do it? (Make a commitment.)

CHAPTER EIGHT

Accelerate Toward Fear

Decide that you want it more than you are afraid of it.

—Bill Cosby

Every now and then I find myself facing a situation where success looks impossible. The odds are clearly not in my favor, but the desire to succeed is compelling. Sometimes it is just the need to succeed that provides the incentive, so I do what I have trained myself to do. I take that first frightening step toward my fear.

Several years ago I decided to test my wilderness survival skills by spending four weeks alone in the wilderness of Arkansas' Ozark Mountains. I will never forget parking my truck down a remote country road and walking off into the wild. My expectations were high . . . until night fell and the thunderstorms began. The first night in the tent was a tough mental challenge. I was alone in the middle of nowhere, miles from another human being. This wasn't feeling like such a good idea now that I was facing the realities. The next morning I had to make a decision: would I stay close to the truck near what was familiar to me or head deeper into the unknown? I'm not proud to say that I packed up and hiked back to the trailhead to the safety of my truck.

I sat in my truck for a few hours, wrestling with the thought of abandoning my dream. Somewhere in the process of that mental battle, I began to focus on the opportunity that lay right before me. I would probably never have this chance again. My courage began to rise. Before I knew it, I made my way out of the truck, put on my backpack, and headed back down the mountain toward the fear and into four weeks of unbelievable memories. Those four weeks ultimately opened the door to *Surf the Woods*, the TrailblazeNow Organization, and even my ambitious search for the remains of Noah's ark. None of these would likely have been possible had I not walked back down into those woods that day.

I have a map now that hangs on the wall in my office. It's filled with the GPS locations of forgotten waterfalls, caves, and old structures throughout the Ozarks, locations I found during those unforgettable four weeks. When I look at that map, I am reminded of something I learned about fear on that trip. When I move toward fear, the door opens to the abundant life. The opposite is also true. Moving away from fear is actually the direction of regret, frustration, and failure. Unless we embrace this truth, we will be sucked toward the safe zone. If we are going to be successful at living our God-inspired dreams, we have got to learn to embrace fear. In fact, we have to look to fear in order to get direction for our journey. This truth brings us to the last of our dreamer's principles.

Dreamer's Principle 4: Accelerate Toward Fear

Some years ago I started thinking about the one life principle that I wanted to sow deep inside my children's hearts, a principle I thought would help them achieve the maximum level of success that God had intended for them. I was not necessarily looking for spiritual principles, although I do believe those are critical. I wanted to go right at the heart of what puts more people in the safe zone than anything else in life. From my experience, the biggest dream killer is fear, so I set out to change the way my children looked at fear. I wanted them to come to embrace fear as the doorway to success and progress in life. The muscle we use to combat fear is courage (or faith); and like all muscles, courage could be strengthened by using it more and more.

I sat down one night and wrote what I call the Dreamer's Creed. I wrote it to help my children, but it has turned out to be the motto for my life as well.

> *I'll go where I'm scared to go,*
> *I'll face what I'm scared to face,*
> *I'll say what I'm scared to say,*
> *To live the dream God has for me.*

It is hard to live according to the words of that creed. My body and mind tell me to avoid situations where I have to exercise courage and faith. Yet the Bible tells me to move toward situations where faith is required if I want to please God (Hebrews 11:6), and live the rewarding life. I see in Galatians 5:16 (HCSB) that my flesh is at war with God's Spirit in my life.

> Walk by the Spirit and you will not carry out the desire of
> the flesh. For the flesh desires what is against the Spirit,

and the Spirit desires what is against the flesh; these are opposed to each other, so that you don't do what you want.

People are not naturally drawn to the risk that comes with moving toward faith. But the Bible promises positive benefits to those who are not ruled by their mind and body (flesh), and instead choose to walk by faith. This requires courage. Frequently, we will have to stare directly into the face of fear. If we let fear grip us, it will knock us down, tie us up, and keep us captive to a safe and ultimately disappointing life.

Think back to the Israelites of the Bible. God saw them suffering in captivity in Egypt. He sent Moses to tell them that He was ready to grant their dream of freedom. I can just hear Moses saying, "Grab your things and follow. God is getting us out of here and taking us to the land He has promised us." They headed out of Egypt and right through the sea, following fire by night and a cloud by day. They encountered miracles all the way to the edge of the Promised Land. They stood at the outer boundary of their dream. They had God's promise and even His presence. The only thing that stood in their way was fear. And they wouldn't take the next step. All they saw were the obstacles that stood in the way. Because of their unwillingness to move *toward* fear, they wandered forty long years in the wilderness.

You may be staring down what appear to be imposing obstacles that stand between you and your dream, and you're hoping to find a way to maneuver around those obstacles. But likely what you actually need to do is move directly toward your fear and over those obstacles. If you get nothing else from this book, please pay attention to the next four sentences: To find victory in your dream journey, start by putting a face on the fear. Then, prepare well for what you can control. Next, relax your grip on what you can't control. And finally, accelerate toward the fear.

Put a face on the fear

When my kids were young, I used to drive them to school each morning. One of our regular routines was to pull out my Bible, read a verse from Proverbs, talk about it, and then pray. It was a great way to work into their lives the practical wisdom found in the Scripture. As they got older, they seemed less enamored with the routine, and what was once a good thing slowly started slipping away. Eventually, I stopped the routine altogether. The Bible was still tucked in my truck visor, but it didn't get used during those fifteen-minute drives to school.

When my oldest son was in his early teens, he and I were riding along together one morning, just the two of us. I thought, *It would be a great time to read a Proverb and pray like we used to do.* Then another thought ran across my mind: *You better not do that; just take the time to enjoy some conversation with your son. After all, you haven't had the chance to spend much one-on-one time with him lately.* I left the Bible in my visor and passed on the opportunity.

Later I realized that I had stared directly into the eyes of fear. It had not occurred to me that I was dealing with a fear issue when I was in the middle of the decision. Rather than seeing it as fear, I had dismissed the situation as a decision between two equally relevant points, and I just picked the one that I thought made the most sense. But playing back the situation in my mind, I knew that the right thing would have been to spend those few minutes in Scripture-reading and prayer with my son. In fact, the more I thought about it, the more convinced I was that God had orchestrated the moment, and it was fear that kept me from following through. I had to ask myself, *What was I afraid of?* And I knew immediately: I was afraid my son would think I was weird. He was a teenager now, and he might start to drift away from me if I showed signs of being super-spiritual. It was clear what I was dealing with. I was dealing with the fear of "What will people think?"

I had put a face on the fear, realizing what was at its core, and I could now more easily work through it. The next day I pulled that Bible from my visor, and my son and I had an excellent discussion about the wisdom of Proverbs. It was just another example of how moving toward fear brings positive results.

At the point where you put a face on fear and look it straight in the eye, you can fight it from the truths found in Scripture. Hopefully, you have memorized a few verses that can be helpful in these situations. (I have listed a few scriptures in appendix 2 that are reliable ammunition for the feeling of fear.) You can also deal with fear by reflecting back on how you overcame similar situations along the journey. Find courage by reminding yourself of God's past faithfulness.

Now, begin moving into fear by preparing well for what you can control.

Prepare well for what you can control

In the wilderness, repelling is one of the skills I have learned and often put to use. I love the feeling that I get when I back up to the edge of a rock wall, lean back in my harness, and start edging down a cliff. I should say that I enjoy the feeling now, but the first time I repelled . . . not so much. That feeling was closer to sheer terror.

Backing over the edge of a cliff is not normal. Common sense tells us that the safe thing to do is to move away from the edge. Why risk it? But common sense eluded me soon after I put on the harness the first time. As I watched my friend Greg tie the rope to a tree and hook me in with a figure-eight device, I desperately wanted to be anywhere but on the edge of that cliff. As Greg coached me over the edge the first time, I held tightly to the rope and quickly made my way down the wall. My goal was to hurry up and get the experience over with. Once my feet hit the ground and I knew I was safe, a feeling came over me that repelling was actually something I could enjoy. I was ready to go again. I could see now that going over a dangerous cliff could be safe as long as you were attached properly to a rope, a harness, and a belay device.

The same principle applies as you are preparing to move into any fear. Whatever the fear might be, always move into it prepared. You want to bring as much confidence as you can to the moment when you confront that fear head on. I would not dream of repelling without a safe rope, a good harness, and a good belay device. That would be foolish. I wouldn't be prepared. But with those devices in place, I can have confidence as I make my way over the edge. Manage all the variables as best you can, and bring strategy to the courageous moment. Bottom line: prepare well for what you can control, and then relax your grip on what you can't control.

Relax your grip on what you can't control

I have battled all my life with wanting to please people. I just hate to disappoint. It started as a child; I never liked disappointing my parents. They likely fueled my fear by heaping too much praise on my good behavior. To make matters worse, I was a preacher's kid. The expectations were even higher for good behavior. Not that my parents ever tried to put pressure on me, but being a people-pleasing child in a family of "professional" Christians added the pressure regardless. My fear as a child and even as a young adult was that I would disappoint my family with some sort of failure. I still battle with this stress as an adult in relation to my friends, employees, and colleagues.

People-pleasers often appear to have a lot of things going their way. After all, life comes a little easier to those who make decisions based on what is going to make the most people happy. Oftentimes people-pleasers are put on a pedestal and they are pointed to as examples of what others should be like. For a while the pedestal feels comfortable.

The people-pleaser may strike a happy pose, but inside he is gripped with worry over what people think of him. At some point, he grows tired of the heavy burden. He wants to climb down from the pedestal, but that's too risky. So he stays on the pedestal until life inflicts a painful blow, and he falls down to reality. And after the fall, he finally gets the clear picture: you cannot control what other people really think about you.

Ironically, that fall eventually brings great relief by causing you to realize that you no longer have to make everyone happy. I have experienced this myself and I can tell you firsthand, handled properly, failure can help relieve you of burdens. You finally learn to relax your grip on what you can't control.

What burdens you? If you can truly say that you have been responsible and have done all you can to work through a difficult situation, yet it persists, you are likely up against something you cannot control. If you've been diligent to prepare well for a fearful or ambitious moment, relax your grip on the outcome. Stress comes, in part, when you try to control what you can't. It is in those cases that you need to open your hands and release your grip. Trust God with the outcome.

When I take someone rappelling for the first time, I often notice that they keep a tight grip on the rope as they descend. This creates a lot of friction and they usually complain about how hot their hands get, even though they are wearing gloves. I explain to them that keeping a tight grip on the rope is a false sense of security. The proper way down is to loosen their grip so the equipment can do the work of managing the descent.

The same is true for those walking their dream journey. When you're up against a fear, put a face on it, prepare to move into it, and relax your grip on the parts of it you can't control. Ultimately you cannot control what people think, but you can work to live a life filled with love. Ultimately you cannot control your health, but you can avoid foods and activities that harm your body. You cannot control whether or not you were born into money, but you can control making the most of what you have. You may not be able to control who your boss is, but you can control your attitude. You cannot control how much mental power you have, but you can make the most of learning. You get the picture. God ultimately is in control of these situations. And the good news is He is our partner in the dream journey. We must face our fears courageously, prepare well for battle, and then stand before the challenge with arms and hands wide open, releasing what we cannot control. That is the posture of those who are living their God-inspired dreams.

Now you are ready to run toward the fight.

Don't Hesitate, Accelerate!

There is a great cave near Jasper, Arkansas, just up from the Buffalo National River. I love this area of my beautiful state. They call the cave Copperhead. I can remember the first time I went to it. A friend had told me about the beauty of Copperhead Cave. He talked about the crystal clear stream that ran through it and the feature that people call the "toilet bowl," a rushing vortex of water that you have to climb through. It all sounded so beautiful, so we agreed to explore it together.

We parked the car along a dusty county road and then made our way into the mountains along a dry creek bed. After a while my friend dropped his pack and pointed down. There in the creek bed was a small hole in the ground underneath a couple of boulders. It was barely big enough for the average size man to squeeze through. I pointed toward the hole in disbelief. "Is this where we go in?" I asked. Sure enough, it was. I leaned over to look into the hole. I could hear the sounds of water moving below, but I couldn't see anything past the two boulders. My friend tied a rope to a tree nearby and dropped the rope down through the narrow passageway and into the darkness. I questioned my courage at that point. Maybe the experience was not worth the effort.

To enter Copperhead, we squeezed through the narrow entrance and then rappelled down 25–30 feet into the middle of a free-flowing creek. I had been to plenty of caves before, but entering a cave on a rope was a first for me. I was putting up a pretty brave front, but in reality I was scared. I hooked myself into the rope and then my friend coached me. I started in and quickly began to back out. He said, "Don't think about it. Just go!" In a matter of minutes I was descending into utter darkness. Finally, my feet touched down in the cold water of the creek. I unhooked the rope and my eyes began to adjust to the darkness. The cave was beautiful. Two hours later I emerged from the cave with one of my favorite wilderness memories of all time. Moving into the fear was well worth the effort.

Whenever you are confused about where you should go next in pursuit of your dreams, prioritize paradoxically and take your direction from fear. Remember to embrace it as a guidepost for where God wants you to travel as He calls you toward the abundant life of faith. Fear points in the direction of progress, but never is it an invitation to be stupid. You would never jump off the Empire State Building just because you are afraid to do it. Use common sense and prepare well to move into fear. Release to God the things you cannot control, and then "don't think about it—just go!" Hesitation gives rise to fear and uncertainty. Proceed boldly and confidently toward your fear with anticipation.

What lies on the other side of each successful battle is an abundant life, your promised land of hope. Time and time again you will see this principle proven true. If you accelerate toward fear, you will experience the rewards of moving your dream further down the road toward its fullness. If you choose to back away from the encounter, you will take a step back toward the safe zone. Test this principle in small doses and see for yourself. Develop your courage muscles by taking small steps of faith. Embrace the Dreamer's Creed and ask yourself each night, "What fear did I walk into today?" Before you know it, you will be a courageous warrior, and you will be moving at supersonic speed along the dream journey.

Fearless

The Lord is my shield.
He goes before me as my guide.
I have no reason to fear.

When I approach the battle,
He holds my sword in His hand.
The victory has already been won.

When I fear, He draws close by my side.
He has patience with my lack of faith,
He understands my frailties.

When I cry out to Him in anger,
He never turns His face from me.
He approaches me with love.

Though all visible circumstances point toward destruction,
I will have faith in Your everlasting love.

I will meditate on Your goodness.
I will dwell on Your promises to care for me.

Though my critics laugh and point out my faults,
My confidence lies in You.

From Your vantage point,
This temporary difficulty has purpose.
It has its place in helping me understand how intimately
You are aware of my every step.

Each time I experience Your faithfulness
My depth of love for You increases.
My fascination with You gains strength.

When I approach a crisis,
I remember Your love and my confidence grows.

Establish in me a powerful spirit of faith, oh Lord.
One that can stand firm in the storm,
That marches forward toward battle,
That welcomes the necessary pain.

Caffeinated Questions

1. What would it look like for you to accelerate toward fear this week?

2. What is a specific, measurable step you could take?

CHAPTER NINE

The Inevitability of Pain

*I firmly believe that any man's finest hour—his greatest fulfillment
to all he holds dear—is that moment when he has worked his
heart out in a good cause and lies exhausted on the field of battle,
victorious.*

—Vince Lombardi

I left Mount Ararat in mid-August 2009, but the dig continued. Six
weeks away from family and work responsibilities had taken their toll
on me. I gave the expedition my best both physically and emotionally.
Now it was up to the remaining American team members and a few
Kurdish men.

The weather window was quickly closing on the mountain. As the men made progress with the dig, negotiations continued for the release of the remaining hostages. It had been approximately four weeks since the PKK had captured the Kurdish and Turkish team members working at the lower site. All but two men had been released, one Kurdish man and one Turkish man. Hopes were high that they would be released soon. I received email reports almost daily about the progress of the dig. Excitement was building, but then tragedy struck. I am not clear regarding all the details, but we were told that one of the two remaining hostages, the Kurdish man, had gotten very sick and needed to be hospitalized. The PKK released him, but killed the Turkish man. Immediately, the Turkish army stepped in and ordered our expedition team off the mountain. The dig was over. If a portion of the ark did lie under the ice cap on the eastern plateau of Mount Ararat, it would be at least one more year before any evidence could be obtained.

I sat back in my chair when I got the news. I was weak from the shock. It took a while for the reality to set in that it had all ended so tragically. I rewound the whole expedition in my mind, and I asked the obvious question. *Why had this all been so difficult?* It went about as bad as it could possibly have gone. We had terrible weather, incomplete supplies, costly delays, less manpower than we were promised, hostages taken, equipment destroyed and, worst of all, someone was killed. Fresh off the news of this tragedy, I told myself I would never return to Mount Ararat. God was working against the effort, not for it. It was over for me. I took my seat in the safe zone.

A few months later I got an email from Richard Bright, the leader of our expedition team. He was planning a return trip in 2010. This man's determination put me to shame. He has made trips to Mount Ararat over twenty-five times in search of the ark, always returning empty handed. He has poured his life's savings into the search. And even though he is in his mid-sixties, he still carries his own backpack.

In 2009, he was near hypothermia after his tent was destroyed near our dig location. He has been ridiculed, insulted, threatened, and injured while pursuing what he believes is his God-inspired dream. Nothing can stop this man's resolve. And even though he has encountered all these roadblocks, he still believes God has called him to the challenge. He won't quit. To paraphrase his philosophy: Why in the world would we expect it to be easy? God is looking for a few men and women who will allow Him to sharpen their character. He knows the timing. Why would we not expect pain in the process?

No matter how hard you work to apply the Four Dreamer's Principles, and no matter how well you practice the trailblazer's rhythms, you will experience pain in the journey. Roadblocks, setbacks, do-overs, slip-ups, and even failures are normal along the trail. As with any ambitious plan, there will be adversity. Hardship happens whenever you journey away from the cozy confines of the safe zone and start blazing new trails toward your God-inspired dreams. It is very important that you normalize the inevitability of pain. If you do this, you will handle the adversity as just another step you must take. Normalize it, and then get ready to fight and endure.

You Have An Enemy – Fight!

The Bible says one of the reasons for struggles is that we have an enemy. The enemy is Satan who wants to derail our plans by taking away our will to succeed. First Peter 5:8 (NIV) reads, "Be alert and of sober mind. Your enemy the devil prowls around like a roaring lion looking for someone to devour."

It should be no surprise that Satan wants to discourage any

individual who is trying to give God lordship over his life. The Bible tells us Satan even tried to discourage Jesus by tempting Him three times when He was alone in the wilderness. No matter how strong you are, you'll be much easier to derail than Jesus. If Satan tried to take Jesus out, you can be sure that you are a target as well, until you take a seat on the sidelines.

Satan's goal is to slam shut the dream door on anyone who is trying to carry out the ambitious work of God. He wants to put them in the safe zone. You must recognize the destructive work of Satan and fight back with the truth of Scripture just as Jesus did.

I fight back by memorizing Scripture. I used to think this was only for preachers and over-zealous Bible beaters, many of whom I cannot relate to personally. But then I tried it and began experiencing the power of this discipline in my own life.

Almost on a daily basis I wake up feeling anxious about some next step I need to take in my dream journey. Often, it's a problem I have to face when I get to work; generally, it involves money. Every two weeks for twenty-four years I've had to make sure I could come up with the money for payroll. Sometimes that's easy. Sometimes it's not. At times like this, Philippians 4:4–8 and Psalm 33:16–19 come to mind. When I am feeling lost in my journey, I think about Psalm 139:1–5. You can find these and other battle verses in appendix 2.

As we see in Ephesians 6:10–18, the Word of God is our sword to use when going on the offensive against Satan. The other weapon is prayer. I have to admit I struggle more with the discipline of prayer than I do with memorizing Scripture. Both are critical, so I continue to work on developing these disciplines by using the technique discussed in the Trailblazer's Rhythm—overload.

There is nothing particularly exciting about memorizing Scripture. Listening to music, watching TV, or surfing the web is definitely more entertaining. It comes down to how badly you really want to live your

God-inspired dream, and how badly you want to live victoriously. If you want to see God do incredible things through your life that only He can do, count on Satan doing whatever he can to discourage you. You are going to need the Scripture ever present in your mind.

You Need Some Training – Endure!

Another equally important reason why we experience hardship when pursuing our dreams is that God wants to develop our character along the way. I love the saying "What doesn't kill me, makes me stronger." Another favorite is "No pain, no gain." There is a lot of truth for the dreamer packed into those two phrases. I think the Bible explains it best in James 1:2–4 (NLT). This has become one of my favorite verses:

> When troubles come your way, consider it an opportunity for great joy. For you know that when your faith is tested, your endurance has a chance to grow. So let it grow, for when your endurance is fully developed, you will be perfect and complete, needing nothing.

I like to paraphrase and personalize the verse like this: Holt, when your endurance is fully developed, you will be strong in character and ready to walk into the fullness of the dream I've given you, but not before. Just have the faith to keep taking steps forward, no matter how small those steps might seem, and I'll keep preparing you.

To gain perspective, I often recall the biblical story about the Israelites and their journey out of Egypt and into the Promised Land. I referred to this in the previous chapter. God did incredible miracles to embolden them and set them free from captivity. Once Pharaoh let them go, God led them on a journey into the wilderness, putting a cloud before them in the day and a pillar of fire before them at night.

He opened up the sea in front of them and destroyed the Egyptian soldiers who were chasing them. He fed them with manna that fell from the sky and gave them water from a rock. Each time they encountered an enemy, God gave them victory. He walked them right up to the Promised Land with miraculous power and might. After all of the miracles they had witnessed, you would think they would have been ready to take any courageous step He asked of them. But, when He asked them to cross over into the Promised Land, they were too fearful. They did not have the character to walk into the fullness of their dream.

Character development comes through the pain of training. But that training is not found in a gym or even in a church. Character gets hammered out through the hardships of life. God knows what is best, and He gives character to those He loves. I have heard it explained this way. If you said to your children, "You can ask me for anything, and I will give it to you." Depending on their age, they might want the latest video game, dream car, or maybe even a million dollars. But if God gave you the opportunity to bless them with any gift that you wanted them to have, most people (if they thought long and hard about it) would ask God to give their children wisdom and character over anything else. Great character is foundational to successful living. The truth is, we don't know what kind of character training is needed before we are ready to walk into the fullness of our dreams. Only God knows. He's the trainer. He has the perfect training regimen. He understands the timing. Our job is to be teachable and to endure the sometimes-painful process.

When I started my business in 1988, I had no idea that God would use Ink as a tool for my character development. Instead, I had visions of piles of money and the freedom of being my own boss. I never envisioned the pain and hardship. That was nowhere in my mind. I didn't want any suffering. If God would have stopped by my tiny apartment personally and talked to me one-on-one about how He was going to use Ink to hammer away at my stubbornness, I would have wanted none of it. He could have explained that He had to start by breaking my pride before I would really have the character to walk into the fullness of any of my dreams. He could have talked about how He needed to develop my faith. I'm sure I would have reasoned with Him that I already had enough faith. As I look back on it now, I have needed every hardship. I have needed every setback. I have needed every failure. Reflecting on my adulthood as a business owner, husband, and father, I can see the refining work He has done on my character through all the trials. I can see the way He has developed my faith. I can see how my desires and ambitions have changed. I can finally start to see what the real calling for my life is. Twenty-four years ago I thought my dream was to build the largest t-shirt printing company in the world. Now that I have walked my dream journey, I have more clarity for how God wants to use me. And I have a bit more character with which He can better use me. I would not trade any of those hammer blows to my character. Pain is inevitable and even good. Endure it.

Beautiful Pain

Pushing forward, ever onward,
Climbing towards the mountain top.
Worn from travel, constant travel;
Painful journey wish to stop.

Scars across me, all inside me;
Memories of a weathered past.
Artwork of this tiresome bushwhack,
Ever on my person last.

Sore from wounds, most recent wounds;
Suffered while the trail I blaze.
Why again this path I travel?
Purpose often shroud in haze.

Looking backwards, sometimes backwards;
see the purpose for the fight.
Thorn-filled jungle once I traveled,
Now a highway towards the Light.

Beautiful pain, purposeful pain;
Hard to see the reasons why.
Broken man who carves the runway,
Does so to help others fly.

Life's a canvas, well worn canvas;
Left behind when grave I lay.
Father's painting, always painting.
Bigger picture clear some day.

Caffeinated Questions

1. What character quality might God be trying to develop in you through your current hardships?

2. How have you seen God use hardships to develop character in your life?

CHAPTER TEN

How Badly Do You Want It?

Twenty years from now you will be more disappointed by the things you didn't do than the ones you did do. So throw off the bowlines. Sail away from the safe harbor. Catch the trade winds in your sails. Explore. Dream. Discover.

—Mark Twain

July 2010: My expedition partners were loading planes to return to Mount Ararat while I sat at my desk and felt sorry for myself. This had been the most emotionally draining season of my life. I was trying to pick up the pieces from the devastation that had come sixteen months earlier. After twenty-two years, my marriage was ending. I hadn't seen it coming. My dream of growing old with my college sweetheart had failed. It seemed fitting that my dream of helping to find the ark should fail as well. I was sure that 2010 would be the year that they would make the discovery, and I wouldn't be there. I was busy attending to my marriage failure. The reasons for this failure fall outside the purposes of this book but rest in part to my not applying some of the principles outlined in the previous pages. I was enduring the consequences of a tragedy I hadn't planned for, but my mind still longed for the Ararat adventure.

Much had been learned in the ark search from the previous mistakes of 2009. This time the team was bringing ground-penetrating radar (GPR) to map the anomaly located under the eastern plateau. GPR would be capable of determining whether there was truly a large man-made structure under the ice. The team still had hopes of digging down to the structure, but after what we had experienced the year before, they were taking no chances. GPR work could be done in a couple of days once they made it back to the eastern plateau. Much money had been given toward the cause, so the pressure was high to come back with some additional scientific data in order to maintain the momentum of this ambitious search.

I had trained all year in hopes of returning. I worked hard to be in even better shape for climbing. I got some additional mountaineering training. I was diligent at learning the Turkish language so I could better communicate with the Kurdish and Turkish team members. I kept studying my wilderness first-responder training books so I would be ready if we had an injury on the mountain. I prepared well for what I could control, but I could not control the family crisis I was going through. Wasn't that supposed to be God's part of the deal? I thought I was following His calling. I just could not understand why He had not fixed this problem. For sixteen long months, I anguished and prayed. He had not handled it the way I thought He should. It ended with a painful divorce. I was frustrated with God.

I received periodic email updates as to the progress on the mountain. The team had two primary goals. One was to take GPR readings on the eastern plateau, and if time allowed, dig down to the structure. The other was to finish the work on the lower site where we had so much trouble with the PKK the year before. They focused first on the lower site, which proved to be a dead end. After completing a comprehensive core sample drilling, they turned up no evidence of the ark. Attention then turned to the GPR work on the upper site. This was a jackpot.

Using the radar, the team found a large object suspended in the stationary ice of the eastern plateau. The object was not ice, and though it was hard, it was not rock. According to the GPR expert, the lines were not consistent with anything found in nature. The expert believed it was likely organic material, and it had to be man-made. The team did not have time to dig for the object, but the trip had been a success nonetheless. They had confirmed what the satellite data had indicated. There did appear to be a large, man-made object underneath the ice cap on Mount Ararat.

I remember opening the email attachment of the post-processed GPR mapping; right there before my eyes seemed to be the shape of a boat. Was I really looking at Noah's ark? It would take at least one more year before we had enough evidence to claim that we had truly found it. We needed wood from this structure, wood that would have to be extracted during the next climbing season. That meant I still had a shot at being there when the ark was discovered. I sat back in my chair and grinned. Maybe my dream was not dead. Maybe God had a better plan. Maybe I needed more character development. Maybe I needed more determination practice.

––––––––––––––––––––

Imagine that you had the ambitious dream to go climb Mount

McKinley, the tallest mountain in North America at 20,320 feet above sea level. You found out from the guide service that you needed to be prepared to carry 40–45 pounds of equipment up the mountain. They told you to expect three weeks of physically demanding climbing at high altitude in extremely cold conditions. If you were serious about tagging the top of Mount McKinley, you would need to train to be in the best shape of your life. After hearing that advice from the guide, it would be stupid to show up at the trailhead hoping to be successful if all you had done to prepare was jog a few miles each day the month prior. If that were the extent of your conditioning plan, you would not reach the top of Mount McKinley. It takes stubborn determination to climb to the top of one of the world's tallest mountains. You have to want it with the kind of desire that will prompt you to punish yourself in preparing. The same is true with living your God-inspired dreams. You have to be in shape for the journey. You need determination conditioning.

Determination is the foundational element of everything I have written about. You can embrace the dreamer's principles and practice the trailblazer's rhythms, but none of that will sustain you. You must possess the kind of determination that prompts you to do whatever has to be done in order to follow God along the journey. The question is and always will be, how badly do you want the dream?

I used to embrace the idea that God would make the road easy for those who were walking according to the call He had put on their lives. After all, if God was behind my idea, it seemed reasonable to think that He would go before me and knock down all the resistance. I was just going along for the ride. These were His ambitious plans, right? But that only makes sense if God has little interest in our character development. God's timetable always makes room for our growth. He is indeed very interested in carrying out the ambitious dreams that He plants in our heart. After all, it is those dreams that bring Him glory. But He will also "slow down" His plans in order to get me involved in a way that allows for my character growth. Unfortunately, that is not the way I tend to lead. Whenever I have an ambitious plan at my company, I try to achieve it in the most efficient way possible. I give little thought to slowing down enough to develop my team members. If I don't think they have the skills or character to carry out my plans at Ink, I quickly start thinking about replacing them with someone better suited for the job. Thankfully, God doesn't lead like I do.

Look at your own life. How have things gone for you this past year? Has it been comfortable? Has it been challenging? How about your energy level? How about your attitude? Your answers indicate, in some respect, whether you are walking an ambitious God-inspired dream journey. If you are following hard after God's plan for your life, it's normal to encounter challenges. You should be exercising determination. Look back again at James 1:2–4 (NLT):

> When troubles come your way, consider it an opportunity for great joy. For you know that when your faith is tested, your endurance has a chance to grow. So let it grow, for when your endurance is fully developed, you will be perfect and complete, needing nothing.

If things have been comfortable for you lately, you should ask yourself whether you are taking the necessary faith steps to follow God's will. The effective dreamer should feel both challenged and energized. The effective dreamer is likely facing difficulties that require determination, yet he is able to maintain a positive outlook. When he lays his head on the pillow at night, he has peace in knowing that he is working out the ambitious dreams God has for his life.

If that is not characteristic of your life right now, you may be growing comfortable in the safe zone. You need determination practice, and that comes in companionship with faith.

It's time to look at our life much like we look at our body. If we want to feel good, look our best, and stay healthy, we have to work against our natural inclinations of doing what comes easily and what feels good at the moment. Unless we work against those inclinations we will sit on the couch, eat junk food, and grow unhealthy and overweight. One day we will wake up and hate the way we look and feel. If we follow our natural inclinations, we won't like the results. If we want to stay healthy, we have to show determination by staying active and making healthy food choices. The lifestyle filled with making tough choices and saying no to what comes naturally gets the results that, in the end, make us happy.

The same is true with living our God-inspired dreams. We may have many ambitious ideas that we want to achieve in partnership with God. We may have wide-open dream doors; and if we apply the principles I've written about, we should be able to get some early momentum. Eventually, though, things will slow down as God allows adversity to come into the picture. He desires to develop our faith in order to make sure we have the character to handle every ambitious leg of the journey He has for us. When challenges come, we will have to reach deep inside ourselves to see how badly we really want the dream.

So, stop making excuses and start training. If you want it badly enough, stick with God's exercise regimen for character development and train with determination. Be faithful.

We can learn a lot about how God views faithfulness from Jesus' story in Matthew 25:14–29 (NIV).

> Again, it will be like a man going on a journey, who called his servants and entrusted his wealth to them. To one he gave five bags of gold, to another two bags, and to another one bag, each according to his ability. Then he went on his journey. The man who had received five bags of gold

went at once and put his money to work and gained five bags more. So also, the one with two bags of gold gained two more. But the man who had received one bag went off, dug a hole in the ground and hid his master's money.

After a long time the master of those servants returned and settled accounts with them. The man who had received five bags of gold brought the other five. "Master," he said, "you entrusted me with five bags of gold. See, I have gained five more."

His master replied, "Well done, good and faithful servant! You have been faithful with a few things; I will put you in charge of many things. Come and share your master's happiness!"

The man with two bags of gold also came. "Master," he said, "you entrusted me with two bags of gold; see, I have gained two more."

His master replied, "Well done, good and faithful servant! You have been faithful with a few things; I will put you in charge of many things. Come and share your master's happiness!"

Then the man who had received one bag of gold came. "Master," he said, "I knew that you are a hard man, harvesting where you have not sown and gathering where you have not scattered seed. So I was afraid and went out and hid your gold in the ground. See, here is what belongs to you."

His master replied, "You wicked, lazy servant! So you knew that I harvest where I have not sown and gather where I have not scattered seed? Well then, you should have put my money on deposit with the bankers, so that when I returned I would have received it back with interest.

So take the bag of gold from him and give it to the one
who has ten bags. For whoever has will be given more,
and they will have an abundance. Whoever does not have,
even what they have will be taken from them."

It takes determination to be faithful. It's much easier to take the
talents and blessings that God has given us and either protect them or
just relax and enjoy them for ourselves. That's what comes natural for
us. It takes determination to be faithful with those same blessings and
make the most out of them.

As you take steps toward your dreams, God is going to be watching
to see how faithful you are with the ambitious plans He has for your
life. Will you do much with what you have, or will you quit? Will you
push forward when life gets busy, or will you quit? Will you forge
ahead when things don't come easy and others tell you to get back to
reality, or will you quit? Will you pick yourself up when something you
try fails, or will you quit? Before you take one step toward your God-
inspired dream, determine to be determined. Be committed to God's
conditioning plan.

Caffeinated Questions

1. How comfortable are you at this stage in your life, and why?

2. Where do you currently have to exercise determination in your life?

3. What is that determination teaching you?

LEAP

CHAPTER ELEVEN

The Power of Your Uniqueness

There is no magic in small plans. When I consider my ministry, I think of the world. Anything less than that would not be worthy of Christ nor His will for my life.

—Henrietta Mears

In the early summer of 2012 our team gathered in Dallas for a pre-expedition planning meeting. Three expeditions to the mountain had taught us much; and while there had been strong hints of a discovery, we had yet to retrieve clear indisputable evidence.

Two thousand nine had been the year of testing. That year we dug a small 20-foot hole that ended up leading to nowhere even though the satellite imagery had indicated an anomaly under the ice cap. That was also the year of relentless mountain storms that impeded our plans, and the year one of our team members was captured and killed by militia forces. I remember it as the year of the "rude awakening" when I realized that finding the ark—if we ever did—would come at a high price.

In 2010 I had gone through a divorce, and as a result was not able to go with the team to Mount Ararat. It was a trying time for me as I sat at home wondering if they would make a discovery without me. Their time on the eastern plateau that year was limited to just two days. Using ground-penetrating radar, two of our team members were able to locate an anomaly underneath the ice. It was only a small slice, but it was all we needed to confirm what satellite data had already hinted at. There was something man-made underneath the ice cap on Ararat.

In 2011, I returned to Ararat. Our team went back to the eastern plateau with the goal of once again using ground-penetrating radar (GPR) to survey a larger portion of the anomaly. We were looking for the shallowest depth of the object underneath the ice. Once we found the shallow point, we planned to cover the area with a work tent and begin digging. We hoped to extract a portion and return it to the States for scientific testing and analysis. We believed that a sample, along with the data from the GPR survey, would be all that was needed to claim we had discovered the remains of Noah's ark. Hopes were extremely high as we surveyed the plateau, but the results left us scratching our heads in confusion. It wasn't clear where we should dig, and our results were not in complete agreement with what we had heard from the satellite operator before we left for the expedition. In the end, we made an educated guess regarding where to set up and dig. But the dig proved fruitless.

In the weeks and months that followed, we evaluated our mistakes and tried to devise a plan for 2012 that would eliminate all the guessing. We decided that it was critical that our GPR team talk live to the satellite team while we were there on the eastern plateau. In the past, those conversations had taken place prior to the team's departure for Turkey. We had always been given approximate GPS coordinates to our dig target. But for some reason, GPS units didn't show accurate coordinates once we were in position on the mountain. We theorized that the Turkish military interrupted signals causing our GPS units problems. Mount Ararat is, in fact, a very sensitive military area. One minute our GPS units would take us to a specific location, only to have the direction indicator point 50 feet in a different direction a few minutes later. The guessing could be eliminated if we could talk to the satellite operator while we were standing on the eastern plateau. At the Dallas meeting, we put all the plans together for the perfect expedition.

The excitement was building within me as the day approached for my return to Ararat. I lay in bed thinking about how my life would change with a discovery. I often asked myself why I was getting this opportunity. *Why not some other follower of Christ who sinned less, read his Bible daily, and prayed more often?* I was the divorced guy with a past that didn't necessarily sit nicely with some Christians.

I thought back to my two previous trips to the mountain, to all those long nights enduring the cold in my sleeping bag. I thought about the incredible journey that had put me in position to be part of the ark search. As a Christian and an adventurer, a dangerous search for the final resting place of Noah's ark was equivalent to a college football player being taken in the first round of the NFL draft. It didn't get any better. I was again willing to endure whatever hardship this mountain could throw at me. I was confident that God had called me for a reason to this point in time. He had designed me specifically for opportunities like this. I knew God had drawn me toward adventures like this, because I had spent time analyzing the unique stories of my life and contemplated what those stories said about how He was shaping me. When I strayed from the adventurous life, I felt unhappy, discontented, and even rebellious. I realized that my life had uniqueness. My stories, strengths, and passions where all designed so that I could execute on the great dreams God wanted to carry out in partnership with me. I was ready to do my part to make this dream a reality. The year we would make the discovery was going to be 2012.

In my experience of counseling others regarding life-effectiveness issues, I have found that many have no clear understanding of what makes them unique and how they can harness that uniqueness to make an impact. Not just any impact, but a unique impact that is inspired and in sync with the way they were designed by God.

Once you understand this powerful concept, you too can partner with God to make a significant impact with your life. And it begins by understanding your story.

Your Unique Story

I find it interesting to read biographies or watch movies about great men and women, past or present. When you place someone's life within the confines of a 200-page book or a two-hour film, it's not difficult to trace his or her greatness back to a few defining circumstances. Sure, there are twists and turns, failures and successes, but it all makes sense once you know the whole story. And like most good stories, these biographies offer lessons of redemption from which we can all learn.

Where are you in the story of *your* life? What chapter are you writing right now? Look closely at the chapters you have already lived. Search for the defining circumstances that have made you who you are today. As you study those circumstances, you will notice how they shaped you in a unique way. Now try and put a title to your life based on the chapters that have already played out. That title will give you a greater understanding of your uniqueness. I refer to that title as your God-inspired name.

Allow me to use my own life as an example. My father was a Baptist preacher and my mom a homemaker. We moved often. My dad would take a church and then struggle to gain positive momentum with the congregation. When I was a young teen, we lived in Memphis, Tennessee. That was the pinnacle of my dad's pastoral career. He was leading a relatively large church in an affluent part of the city. Over the course of four years, I watched as the church struggled with turmoil under his leadership. It culminated with the church asking him to step down. As a result, we moved to a little town in southern Arkansas where my dad pastored a small church, a far cry from the large church in Memphis. Yet the following four years proved similar in that this church also grew divided under my dad's leadership. When I was eighteen years old, that church also voted in favor of his resignation. That was the last pastorate my dad ever had. He slid into a deep depression and never truly recovered. He spent the next twenty-five years addicted to medication that dulled his depression and anxiety. My mother eventually left him. I think it is safe to say he never fully experienced his God-inspired dream.

I can remember watching my dad as he led those congregations. He didn't appear to be successful as he walked the steps of his career. The disappointment I'm sure he felt was not just confined to him. My mom, my sister, and I all felt it as well. But I think something went a little deeper with me. As a son, I kept a close eye on my father for direction in life. As far as a career went, his appeared to point toward failure, not the direction I wanted to go.

As a young man, I asked myself how I was going to be different. I decided that I would find out what I did well and then pursue it relentlessly. No matter how hard I had to work at success, I was going to find it. These, I believe, were the circumstances in my story where God wrote a redeeming word across my life, the word *determination*. The circumstances of my father's life proved sad. But God touched me through those circumstances and inspired me toward a rewarding life that has given me the opportunity to touch others in a positive way. In many ways, right or wrong, my father's example proved to be the fuel for my determination.

Your Unique Strengths

We all have strengths. What is not often obvious is how powerful our strengths can be when we work in harmony with our story and our passion.

Strengths, in this context, are those things that make *you* uniquely *you*. They are the things that come most naturally to you, the tools in your unique design that you tend to rely most heavily on when working to accomplish a task. Often my strengths involve working with my hands and using my body. I also have strengths in the area of casting vision. I have grown in my understanding of these strengths by doing several things:

- I've analyzed my successes and failures.
- I've gotten objective feedback from those who are close to me.
- I've taken several diagnostic tests to gain perspective.

It is critical that you do the same if you are serious about walking successfully into your own God-inspired dreams. Start by looking back over your life. Take some time to chart your successes and failures and ask yourself why. What made you successful in those endeavors? Why the failures? What starts to emerge is a more objective understanding of what you are good at and what you are not so good at.

Again, using my life as an example, I very much enjoy working with my hands, and I have always enjoyed outdoor activities that involved putting my body through rigors that test the limits of my stamina. When I was a teenager, I gravitated to long-distance running and weight lifting. As I got older, I started backpacking, climbing, mountaineering, and testing my endurance with wilderness survival. I not only enjoy participating in these activities, but I also enjoy reading everything I can on these subjects in order to get better. Bottom line: I am energized when I put my body through rigorous physical activity. But that is not the case with my mind. I struggle to sit still through long conversations and long-winded speakers. I want to be out using my body. My hands and my body are core strengths for me.

When I have talked to other people about my strengths, they've pointed me toward the leadership roles in my life. Close friends have reminded me that whenever I become a part of an organization or a team, I tend to hold the reins of leadership. In most cases, I didn't seek the leadership role, it was offered to me. My closest friends have told me they think this has to do with my strength of vision. They say that I appear to know where I'm going, and where I'm going is usually toward an exciting destination. My vision is another core strength God has given me.

When trying to gain insight about your strengths, I recommend you take some personality profiles that will help you see objectively how you are wired. I have found that they provide informative feedback. Examples include the Meyers/Briggs, DISC, Birkman, and StrengthsFinder assessments. I have taken many of these. One I really like was developed by a couple of friends of mine, a profile called 3:9 Principle. This particular assessment helps you understand your innate aptitudes and natural bent. Through the lens of the 3:9 Principle you will learn your unique design and how it shapes the way you approach life.

Your Energizing Passion

Passion is the fuel that gives you energy, the underlying cause behind why you enjoy doing whatever it is you really enjoy doing. Often when I ask people what they are passionate about, they talk about such things as saving the planet, politics, or even their favorite sports team. Those are not the passions I am referring to in this context. Saving the planet could be an example of a cause you feel strongly about, but it is not an example of what I call an energizing passion. It is important that you identify your distinct energizing passion, because it is often in that context where you will best carry out your God-inspired dreams. If your vision is in association with a passion that energizes you personally, you will have the determination necessary to continue to push your dream along as you inevitably come up against setbacks, delays, and obstacles.

I don't have to look hard to find my passion. Just ask me what energizes me, and I will tell you adventure. But it is not just wilderness adventure that energizes me. It's any occasion where I get to blaze a unique trail in my life. My business is a perfect example. As an entrepreneur, I blaze new trails everyday. Therefore, I'm energized most days. I like the challenge that comes with charting new territory as long as I have some great individuals with me in support of those efforts. I have enjoyed some prosperous times and endured some nearly bankrupt times, but I have always had the energy because being a small business owner falls within my passion for adventure. What do I do when I am tired and frustrated with work or family issues? I go to the wilderness to look for adventure. Adventure is my energizing passion.

What is the energizing passion of your life? Ask yourself what gives you energy. What drains your energy? Think through situations when you are interacting with others. List these energizing activities on paper; then next to each one, answer the question *why*. For instance, if you are energized by solving problems at work or working puzzles at home, the *why* might be because your energizing passion is problem solving. Maybe you like to sit down over a cup of coffee and talk with people one-on-one. Your energizing passion could be conversation. If you find that you really enjoy being involved in sports, your energizing passion may be competition.

Take time to understand the unique story, strengths, and energizing passion of your life. They will provide inspiration and direction for you as you wrestle with the great dreams God is calling you toward.

Caffeinated Questions

1. What one or two words would you use to summarize the story of your life?

2. Why did you choose those words?

3. What have people told you are your greatest strengths?

4. What activities in your life give you the most energy?

5. Why do these activities energize you?

CHAPTER TWELVE

Take the LEAP

Dream no small dreams. They have no power to stir the souls of men.

—Victor Hugo

On August 6, 2012, my plane touched down in Van, Turkey. I was already feeling the jet lag as I made my way to the luggage carousel. I had accompanied John, the ground-penetrating radar expert from Dallas. John is a highly regarded expert in his field, and I was honored that he wanted me to escort him to the top. I was thinking about his wife's last words when I saw her in Dallas: "Make sure you get him up and down safely." If only she knew how intimidated I was myself by the rugged power of Mount Ararat. It was hard enough getting myself up and down the mountain safely, much less taking responsibility for others. But somehow I had become the team's mountaineering expert, a title I wore with reluctance because I knew that real mountaineers would scoff at my credentials. Regardless, I did have more experience than most and my physical strength as a climber had earned me the title of Little Horse by the Kurdish porters on the team. As John and I made our way out of the terminal and to the waiting car, I could see the excitement building on his face. If he was confident about our mission, I had reason to be confident as well.

We started up the mountain on August 8. My initial job was to get John safely to the summit by August 11. It was critical that I have him there on that day because the live conversation—via satellite phone— was scheduled to take place between him and the satellite technician the following morning. We had timed it such that the satellite would be passing overhead at that time and would have full view of the eastern plateau. John had a special chip in his satellite phone that the operator could detect. The plan was for the operator to locate John in relationship to several shallow portions of the anomaly under the ice cap. He would then give John directions on where he was in reference to those shallow points. John would move into proper position and then flag the shallow points. If all went well and the weather cooperated, we estimated we would have accurate locations to several shallow points plus or minus only a few feet.

John and I reached the 14,000-foot approach camp on August 9, and it became apparent to me that my plans were going to have to change. The baggage and supplies for the high camp were beginning to build up at the approach camp. The Kurdish porters had been hired to carry supplies each morning up the difficult summit route to high camp and then return for another load the following morning. The problem was, they didn't know how to prioritize their loads. Some of the items that

I knew to be vital to our success at high camp were not being shuttled to the top, while things we wouldn't need for days or even weeks were being taken first. There was no leadership at the approach camp, and I was going to have to provide it. So, on the morning of August 11, I guided John to the summit in time for the following day's satellite call; and after a short meeting with the summit team, I made my way back down to the approach camp. There I would direct the Kurdish effort until arrangements could be made for someone to replace me.

On August 12 the weather cooperated and I got word that the plan had worked flawlessly. The satellite conference call proved successful and the team flagged several locations across the ice for evaluation with ground-penetrating radar (GPR). In the days that followed, the summit team pulled the GPR units across the ice cap to map the anomaly and confirm the shallow-point depths that the satellite had identified. The limited news I had received from the summit team was that the results were amazing. I waited anxiously at the approach camp for the day John was to return. *Had we finally found the ark?* My mind drifted toward that possibility. I lay in my tent at night dreaming about how much my life would change if that were the case.

It had been five days since I left the team at the summit and climbed back down to manage the porters. This was the day John was to return with a couple of our Kurdish team members. I stared up at the rugged summit trail that leaves the approach camp and marks the four- to five-hour climb to Mount Ararat's ice-capped peaks. I wondered what stories the team would tell on their return. If the GPR evidence pointed strongly toward a find, and if they had been able to hit the object with the drills at the reported depths, I would move on up to the top and begin helping to lead the dig team. Our job would be to dig an 8x8-foot hole down to the object and extract a piece for scientific research and analysis.

The morning wait held me captive until nearly noon. Finally, off in the distance I spotted them as they slowly made their descent. The suspense was too much. Rather than wait for them to climb down to me, I started up the mountain to meet them. When I got within fifty yards of John, I could see a big smile spread wide across his face. "We found it! We found it!" he yelled. It was just what I had longed to hear after four painful years of searching. I climbed up to him and we hugged with excitement. As we made our way down to the approach camp together, John went into great detail about how the satellite depths had matched with the GPR results. He talked about how they drilled for the anomaly at the shallow point of 34 feet. When they drilled to that depth, the diamond-bit ice core got stuck in the object at just beyond the 34-foot mark. They were unable to retrieve the drill bit, and it had been left sticking out from the ice. He and the rest of the team saw this as further evidence that we were in fact preparing to dig in the proper location.

Most impressive of all was what he said about the 3-D GPR results. He said you could clearly see the hull of the ship. You could see the decks and even the compartments. He was so confident in the find that he was convinced we should publish the radar results even if we were not able to reach the object with the dig. His confidence was contagious. I didn't care how hard it was going to be, we were going to be successful with the dig. John left the mountain and returned to the United States. A couple of days later, I made my way up to help lead the dig effort.

———————————

People often ask me how I ever came to be involved in such an incredible opportunity as being a lead mountaineer in the ark search effort. While pursuing the God-inspired dreams of my life, I have discovered that what seems impossible is often very possible after all. The power to move toward the seemingly unrealistic goal of finding

Noah's ark came, in part, as a result of understanding the calling that I believe God has stamped across my life. I have discovered this calling by going through a process I call LEAP, an acronym I find helpful when coaching individuals:

Learn your story.
Explore your strengths.
Aim for your God-inspired dream.
Pursue your next step.

Effective dreamers LEAP. They understand their story and where it's pointing them in life. They understand how God has created them uniquely and with specific strengths and passions. They maintain momentum toward their goals by breaking their ambitious journey down into small steps forward, and then they focus on pursuing the very next small step. You may wonder: How do they know where to aim? How do they differentiate between a God-inspired dream and a calling? How do they come up with ambitious dreams in the first place? These are great questions.

There is an important distinction between your God-inspired dreams and your calling. Some might substitute the words *life mission* for calling. I prefer *calling* because I believe it more accurately represents the power of God's pull across our lives toward His plans and not our own. After all, it's God that gave us our strengths and passions. It is God who shapes our story through His hand of grace in our lives. It is God who made us who we are, and it is God who should get the glory for any impact that we may have with our lives through the dreams He has given us and the calling He has placed upon us.

To understand the difference between a God-inspired dream and a calling, let's look at what I call the dream arrow.

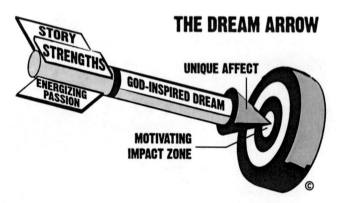

THE DREAM ARROW

The arrow represents a unique dream that God has given you. Effective dreamers typically have more than one God-inspired dream, each given by Him for a distinct purpose. These dreams should reflect your story, strength, and energizing passion. And they should make sense in relation to your motivating impact zone and the unique affect you have on the impact zone. In short, your motivating impact zone is the people group, or in some cases the cause, that you naturally have a desire to impact. Do not expect God to call you to a target for impact without also giving you a naturally occurring desire to make a difference there. Your unique effect is the distinct way you personally affect the target, or the way it responds to you.

Unlike your actual dreams, your calling is more like the quiver that holds the dream arrows. Each arrow is distinct, but all are unified by a common theme—your calling.

Let's use my life as an example.

My story:	Determination
My strengths:	Working with my hands, pushing my body to its limits, and inspiring vision
My energizing passion:	Adventure
My unique effect:	Igniter
My motivating impact zone:	Ministry to men

There are several different dream arrows in my life that God continues to sharpen for impact. These arrows reflect my LEAP profile.

- Dream 1:   Build an inspired team at my business
- Dream 2:   Use wilderness experiences to impact men through a nonprofit organization
- Dream 3:   Impact men through books, seminars, and retreats
- Dream 4:   Impact the world for Christ by helping to uncover the truth about the final resting place of Noah's ark.

All of these arrows fit nicely into a common calling for my life: helping people resist the pull toward complacency.

Your Calling

What is your calling? Are you maximizing your calling in partnership with God? These questions are more accurately answered once you have spent time working through your LEAP profile. You may already be pursuing some ambitious goals, but if those goals are not in harmony with your unique LEAP profile, you will never find real contentment in your efforts. God designed you a certain way, in order to use you in a certain way, so that He could have an impact in a certain way, to a certain group or cause.

To help you gain insight regarding your calling, ask yourself the question, What parting advice would I give my family if I were on my deathbed? Our whole life is a collection of lessons. We often think those lessons are random, but there is actually a Teacher who is sovereign over our lesson plans. God has those lesson plans in place for a reason; essentially, He is shaping our lives toward a calling.

Your calling should be specific. If, for instance, your calling is to help underprivileged children understand the love of Christ, you would not shape a God-inspired dream around wilderness ministry to men. That would not be in line with your calling. On the other hand, you might create an ambitious plan to minister to an impoverished neighborhood where many children do not have good father figures. That would make sense. Also, you do not want to get too nebulous with your calling because that will give you very little direction. For instance, if you said your calling was to reach the world for Christ, anything goes. That is a poorly crafted calling. You will have little direction with such a broad statement.

Your God-Inspired Dreams

Once you start to understand your calling, it's time to begin thinking specifically about your God-inspired dream(s). Use your calling as the basis for each dream. Again, it all starts by creating your own LEAP profile. (I have provided a LEAP profile worksheet in appendix 3.) Your story, strengths, and passion are the ingredients that should shape your most effective dreams. It would rarely make sense to call something a God-inspired dream if it doesn't reflect the unique way God designed you. Crafting a relevant God-inspired dream is a process that, in my opinion, is 100 percent God inspired and 100 percent hard work. Do not take a passive approach. I am no theologian, but I will write from my own experience and from what I have found in Scripture. God honors our hard work when it is in concert with His inspiration. I would never expect God to bless my business with success if I were not a hard worker and neglected to do my best. When I honor God with my best efforts, I see positive results. The opposite is also true.

Many in the church are not experiencing the fullness of what God wants to do through their lives. People often say they are having little impact because God hasn't given them an ambitious dream. Many tell me something to the effect of, "If God wanted to do something big through my life, He would wake me up one day with a vision for it." Don't use the lack of creative vision as an excuse to limit God's impact through your life. I believe two legitimate questions to ask are, (1) Are you working hard enough to find God's inspiration? and (2) Are you recognizing God's inspiration when He places it before you? Maybe you've just grown complacent. Maybe you need to cut the lock off your dream door and see what's inside. If you lack the vision to craft a compelling God-inspired dream, pray for it and seek advice from other dream-door openers. Do not make excuses. Work hard at exploring for God's vision as it pertains to your life. Pray for clarity and seek advice. God honors that kind of effort, and over time I believe He will build a quiver full of dream arrows with your name etched on each one.

Finally, when it comes to effectively executing God-inspired dreams, I find that there is a balance between waiting on God and taking responsibility. Many Christians operate from what I call the passive perspective. If their business goes bust, marriage falls apart, church goes down the tubes, or they lose their job, they say something like, "I guess God had another plan for me. He is the one in control. I just have to trust Him." In my opinion, we find both truth and deception wound throughout that statement.

It's true that ultimately God is in control, and we are called to trust Him. The problem is, we also need to make sure that we are being responsible. God teaches us that throughout Scripture. Read through Proverbs, for example, and you will get a heavy dose of the importance of being responsible. Or, read through Christ's teaching in the Gospels, especially the parables, where He often talks about being responsible. We are always called to take responsibility for our actions and the consequences that result. We are not supposed to be prideful when good things happen, but it is okay to be happy when your hard work pays off. The opposite is also true. We should be careful not to point the finger at God or anyone else when bad things happen as a result of our actions. Be responsible by always giving your best effort to discover your God-inspired dreams and effectively execute them.

Caffeinated Questions

1. What is the people group or cause that you have a natural desire to impact, and why?

2. What parting advice would you give your family if you were on your deathbed? Explain how or why this advice has come to be important to you.

CHAPTER THIRTEEN

Why Try?

Nobody grows old merely by living a number of years. We grow old by deserting our ideals. Years may wrinkle the skin, but to give up enthusiasm wrinkles the soul.

—Samuel Ullman

On August 28, 2012, I lay inside my sleeping bag with the zipper pulled all the way up and my head tucked deep inside. The cold seemed to slice though the tent and go straight for my feet. I had icicles where my toes used to be. It had been a cold few weeks on Mount Ararat, but that couldn't cool my enthusiasm. Ten years of research, four years as a member of the ark search team, three trips to Ararat, and ten summit climbs were about to pay off. All the sacrifices I had made to stay in shape, train, and gain experience as an outdoorsman made perfect sense in light of what was happening the following day. We had spent the last ten days digging an 8x8-foot hole down to a depth of 32 feet. The following morning we would excavate the final two feet of ice lying between us and the greatest archeological find in history: the remains of Noah's ark.

As I lay there the night before, I thought about my youngest child, Mary. Three out of the last four years I had missed her birthday in favor of this crazy dream of finding the ark. She had turned ten the day before. I lay there wondering about what she had done on her birthday. I wondered if she missed me, or if she had grown so used to my missing her birthdays that it hardly mattered anymore. *Did she really understand the significance of this adventure I was on? Would it all make sense once I put that piece of wood in her hand, a piece of wood from the remnants of Noah's ark?*

Those long nights spent lying in the tent are the worst part of these expeditions. There's a loneliness that almost overwhelms. That particular night my thoughts lifted me 50 feet above my tent where I could see myself protected from frozen death by nothing more than two layers of thin nylon and a down sleeping bag. Then I soared to 1,000 feet, where I could see the headlamps at the lower elevations of the mountain. I wondered if it was the militia forces of the PKK. Off to the east I could see the lights of Iran, a dangerous country for an American. I was a speck out of place in a far off land where people like me go missing, never to be heard of again. My thoughts lifted yet higher, to the stars. I could see the earth turning. I saw Turkey, then the United States, then Arkansas, and finally my house in the little community of Maumelle. Inside I watched my youngest daughter blowing out her birthday candles. Everyone was smiling and laughing, but I was missing from the picture because at that moment I'm halfway around the world on a frozen piece of earth called Mount Ararat. Though the loneliness is almost unbearable, I tell myself again that it will all be worth it tomorrow when we uncover a priceless piece of history.

The dig plan had been simple in theory. The ice drill bit had gotten stuck 34 feet down and was sticking out from the ice by about a meter. According to the satellite and GPR results, this was the shallowest depth to reach the anomaly so this proved the best place for the dig. We marked out the dig parameters around the drill bit and assembled a large tent over the site. Then we erected a pulley system over the dig area, and began using chainsaws and heavy slam bars to slowly excavate the area. With the saws, we cut each layer into 40–50 ice blocks that were approximately ten inches thick. We used the slam bars to break up the sections, which we lifted and placed in baskets that were then hauled up by the pulley system and dumped outside the tent. The drill bit came apart in one-meter sections. Our goal was to celebrate the day's progress by removing one section of the drill bit before we finished that day's work.

After ten days of backbreaking work in extremely cold conditions, we reached the 32-foot depth. There had been some debate that day as to whether we should go ahead and work into the night since we were only two feet away from exposing the last section of the drill bit and having the chance to see what it was actually stuck into. Being that close to realizing one of the great dreams of our lives, it was hard to put the brakes on. But after some discussion, we decided it would be best to wait until morning when the light would be better for filming and documenting this great find. We didn't want anything to go wrong.

So there I was lying in my tent on the eve of this great discovery. My mind was racing. *What would it look like? How hard would it be to cut through?* We had discussed in some detail the risks of taking

samples of the ark out of the country. We had decided to work with the
Turkish authorities on the find. But for those of us who wanted it, it
was worth the risk to chance it with airport security by taking a small
portion of the ark out of the country in our baggage. In fact, there
was some debate as to whether this would even qualify as a prohibited
archeological item since we had no evidence that this truly was the ark.
Testing would first have to be completed on the samples and all the
analysis would have to confirm the hypothesis. For all anyone knew,
it could just be a piece of wood or rock. I thought the risk was well
worth the reward but couldn't help thinking about what it might be
like to be locked away in one of the nasty Turkish prisons I had heard
about. I was going to keep my sample fairly small—one medium-sized
piece to be used for my talks and five small pieces for each of my kids.
I could see no problem getting a small sampling through security. If
questioned, I would say it was something I brought back as a souvenir
from my climb up Mount Ararat. Surely they would accept that as a
reasonable response.

The morning of discovery came on with a beautiful sunrise over the
eastern edge of the mountain. Light poured through the tent. I woke
up and wrote a few thoughts in my journal. I wanted to keep those
feelings fresh for all time. I reasoned that my kids would one day look
back on this moment and would want to know what my thoughts were
at the time.

8/29/2012 journal entry

I lie in the tent this morning thinking about the magnitude
of what's about to happen today. We are two ice layers
down to the top of the ark. It's taken ten long years of
research, relationship building, training, trial-and-error

expeditions, suffering and pain to get to this moment. I wonder what it will look like. What will it feel like to touch it? How hard will it be to extract a piece? My life takes another turn after this moment. There is a new story to tell, a new adventure to go on. I praise God for the path He put me on. I will honor Him with this story.

That morning we all gathered in the meal tent before heading over to the dig site. The word had begun to leak out into the ark search community that a find was eminent. As a result, people from past expeditions were making their way up the mountain in order to be part of this momentous event. My mountaineering friend Kevin DeVries had arrived a few days before. Two other men arrived just after breakfast. Spirits were high as several men shared verses of Scripture that seemed to fit the occasion. Some talked about how God had taught us much the previous few years about faith as we had pursued His calling to locate the ark. One or two of the men prayed for us, and praised God for the wonderful opportunity He was giving us to uncover such a significant piece of biblical history. We shared thoughts about how this discovery could impact the world and rock the unbeliever's concept of God and the Bible. Surely God Himself had ushered us to this moment. It was time for the greatest archeological find in all of history. We made our way over to the dig site.

Dr. Randall Price, our chief archeologist from Liberty University, was the first to make the long descent by rope ladder into the hole. The camera man went next. Randall taped a segment of video regarding the work that had been done up to that point. I climbed into the hole along with one other man, Thomas. Our job would be to cut and remove the final two feet of ice. After so many years of preparation and so much disappointment on previous expeditions, I wanted to be in the hole when the discovery was actually made.

Everyone else gathered above on all sides of the 8x8-foot opening. There were cameras pointing down from all directions. The last drill bit stood up from the bottom of the hole by a couple of feet. Thomas started the chainsaw and we worked to remove the first layer. Within minutes it was gone. Then, only ten inches or so were left between our hands and the ark. Thomas handed me the saw, and I plunged the blade into the ice, anticipating the feeling of it touching down on something that would likely have the texture of rock. But I felt nothing unusual. As I worked my way around, I reasoned that the drill was stuck a little deeper than we thought. Someone grabbed the drill bit and wiggled it back and forth. To my surprise it fell right over. I picked it up and looked in the diamond blade ice core that was attached to the end. I expected it to be full of something resembling wood or rock. To my surprise, it was packed solid with ice. No one said a word.

During moments like that your mind plays tricks on you. It wants what it wants. We had spent the last ten days working in horrible conditions with little sleep and limited food in order to get to this moment. Hundreds of thousands of dollars had been raised over the past several years. Many people had been put in harms way; one life had been lost. But at that moment no one had anything to say. We reacted as if what we were seeing wasn't really happening. I fought the silly urge to stand the drill bit up and put it back in the hole as if no one had seen it fall over. I didn't want to be attached to the bad news that was playing out before us.

After a few moments of silence, Thomas and I resumed digging. We reasoned that even though the satellite and GPR data had placed the object at this depth, they could have been off by a couple of feet. We dug two more layers down. Still nothing. We then thought that perhaps the data on depth had been substantially off. We had the ice drill lowered down into the hole, along with 12 feet of drill bits, and began poking holes all around the base of our dig site. Again, nothing.

The cameras were turned off and the disappointment started to sink in. I made my way out of the hole physically and emotionally drained. It was one of the lowest moments of my life. Only minutes earlier, I had crawled down into that hole expecting to experience one of the high points of my life. I made my way back down Mount Ararat that day. Four years of worked seemed a waste.

Have you ever had a disappointing ending to an exciting goal you hoped to accomplish? Have you ever experienced the kind of failure that makes you ask, Why even try? I was sure asking that question over and over again as I made my way down Mount Ararat and flew back home to the United States. I had also asked that question several times in my life while facing business failures and the pain of divorce. Living an ambitious life puts you at risk for greater disappointment. Is it really worth it?

This brings us to the final component of the dream arrow. In fact, it is the most important component because it is the power behind the arrow. I am talking about the archer, the one who holds the bow and desires to fire the dream arrows of your life.

For those of you in the church community who are reading this, do not get ahead of me here. I have a feeling that many of you are already drawing conclusions about the archer. If you are thinking that it is God who is supposed to hold the bow and shoot the arrows, you are right. But it is not yet time to close the book. This chapter is to you, a believer. I have some important questions for you, so bear with me.

If you do not have a personal relationship with Jesus Christ, this chapter is really not going to make a lot of sense. I am indeed concerned about you, though. Walking successfully in your God-inspired dreams presupposes that God is the most important part of the equation. Your dreams without His influence will never fully satisfy. Many of the principles in this book will help you be more successful in achieving goals, but those goals apart from His plans are just dead ends that will never truly fulfill. In appendix 4, I have given some information on how to enter into a rewarding personal relationship with Jesus Christ. Speaking from personal experience, I would be lost and aimless without the daily power I get in friendship with Jesus. I hope you won't put this book away until you have settled the most important issue for surfing life successfully. Do you know Jesus personally?

The final question to you who are Christians is: Who actually holds the bow? If you are a Christian, we both know it should be God. But in reality, when God actually reaches out to grab your bow, does He have to pry your fingers off the grip? I have to ask myself this question almost daily. I say with my mouth that I want God to be in control, but deep down I still want to hold the bow. I want to shoot the arrows. I want my dreams to go according to my plans, my timing, and hopefully with the least amount of hardship. When things don't go my way, I ask myself, *Why even try?* I want to find the ark when I want to find it and preferably with the least amount of pain. It has taken a lifetime for me to make much headway with this issue, but little by little I have seen God pry my fingers from the grip and lovingly place His hands there.

It comes down to a control issue. I know in theory that God would be the better archer. I can see that from the truths in Scripture. Why can't I give Him the bow? When I try to get to the root of this problem, I come down to two reasons: (1) Faith—I don't trust that His way is without hardship. What if His plan puts me in a position to get hurt? (2) Pride—I have too much ego to let Him have control. What if His plan makes me look bad? What if I don't get the credit if things go well?

I am discovering that these two reasons keep God from being able to use my life to the fullest.

The two things that I am afraid of are in fact the things I need to welcome in order to be more effective at living my God-inspired dream. First of all, I need to embrace hardship's role in developing the faith and character needed to do the great things God has envisioned for me. And second, I need to move over and give God the credit. I don't typically handle success too well anyway. In my case, it usually takes some humbling circumstances in order for me to gain the proper perspective on who really deserves the credit.

I have noticed that God has to take the bow out of my hands by allowing hardships in my life. It is those same hardships that often affect my pride and knock me off the pedestal. The same pedestal where I once sat to receive credit for all the great work I felt I had done in pursuit of my dreams. Few may have noticed the pride. I can play humble with the best in the business. But the closer I come in relationship to Christ, the more I notice the glaring sin of pride.

Earlier in the book I talked about how I used blue-collar goal setting to change the culture of my business. One thing that I didn't address was how I began working my faith into my business. It took hardship and humility for me to do that. For the first twenty years, I kept my faith a fairly private issue around the office. I used the excuse that I didn't want to make people think that I only wanted Christians working at Ink. I told myself that I was using the relational approach to evangelism. My life was an example, but I kept my words pretty much to myself when it came to Christianity. This had an interesting affect in relationship to the pride issue. When I wasn't acknowledging God in front of my employees, it was easier for me to passively take credit for the success of the company. I could occasionally throw up a quick prayer of gratitude at the Christmas party, just to make sure I was covering all the Christian bases, but my faith wasn't at the heart of Ink's culture. It was definitely not in a prominent place for all to see and acknowledge the Power behind the plan. Admittedly, I didn't realize this was what I was doing at the time, but I can look back and see it clearly now.

In 2008, God began to pry my grip from the bow. He allowed financial hardship to begin creeping back in. Like many businesses, the economic recession began to take its toll on Ink that year. We needed God's help more than ever if we were going to survive. I was hitting my knees everyday asking God for guidance on how to lead and how to cash flow through this tough economic drought. It is a lonely place as a leader when you realize that the pedestal you once sat on to feel the applause is now the place where people look with fear. I could almost sense their questions: "What are you going to do now?" "Am I going to lose my job?" I have to give my business partner, Scott, much of the credit here because he shared in most of this burden. He had to carry on the daily duties of running the nuts and bolts of the business, which included hiring, firing, and trying to find a way to pay the bills.

It was during this low point that I came to understand that I had been holding the bow at Ink. I needed to turn it over to more capable hands, the hands of God. To begin changing this I started a weekly Monday morning meeting. The overarching purpose of that meeting was to tie my faith to the mission of the company and to relinquish ultimate control of the business to God while in front of the team. Scott and I do this each week now with a relevant story, scripture, and prayer. The whole thing only takes about ten minutes, but it has dramatically changed the culture. The employees nicknamed the meeting "church." I love it, and from the feedback I get, they seem to love it too. It is interesting looking back on it now; I always thought that I was letting God lead my business. After all, I was privately plugged into Him through prayer and Bible reading. But it was only after I made a very deliberate effort to publicly acknowledge His leadership in the daily workings of the business that I believe He chose to take control.

I still have a mental picture of that first "church" meeting. As I talked to the team members, I could actually picture myself stepping off the pedestal so that God could take His proper place. I took a small step back in pride, and He took a huge step forward in control. As you pursue the fantastic dreams that God will lay on your heart, I encourage you to ask Him daily to root out your pride and replace it with true humility. Remember, those who achieve great things often stumble over those same things because of pride. Get it right by getting out of the way. A great little verse to memorize on the topic is James 4:6 (ESV), "God opposes the proud, but gives grace to the humble." Don't work in opposition to God by neglecting to address the issue of pride in your life. Let go and give Him the bow. Then test for success by asking the following questions.

- Have I searched hard to understand how God designed me for impact?
- Have I given my dreams my best effort creatively?
- Have I worked hard to maintain positive momentum?
- Have I given God control of the bow?

Check for pride by asking:

- Why do I want this dream so badly?
- Am I okay if the outcome looks different from what I had envisioned?
- Am I okay if someone else gets the credit?
- Am I okay with failure if that's what God allows?

I love how Helen Keller puts the daring life in perspective: "Life is a daring adventure or nothing. Security does not exist in nature, nor do the children of men as a whole experience it. Avoiding danger is no safer in the long run than outright exposure." This, in part, answers the question, Why try? As Christians we know that the cause of Christ is certainly worth the effort, and the effort is what makes life rewarding regardless of the outcome.

As of this writing, I still don't have the answers as to what went wrong on the 2012 Mount Ararat expedition. Disappointing as it was for me, my dream of finding the remains of Noah's ark is not over. I am coming to peace with the possibility that I may never find the ark, but the passion for the search still burns within me, so I will continue to give it my very best effort. I am committed to the search until I can clearly see that God has closed the door to this dream He awakened in me.

I realize that I will likely never have the biggest custom t-shirt printing company in America, but I am going to do the best I can with what I have. I understand the possibility that this book may never be read by many, but I will promote it with passion. Also, I may never have a large, growing ministry to men, but it won't be for lack of trying.

The bottom line is I will never regret living an ambitious life, and you won't either. I don't know what your dreams are, but I pray God chooses to bless both of us. Stay in close connection to God while you dream large, work large, and live large. You will never regret a life lived in pursuit of your God-inspired dreams. Now go out and surf the woods!

My List

When I was younger, I used to pray,
"Use my life, Lord, in any way."
But inside my heart He heard me say.
"Here's a list, God. Pick away."
Doctor, Lawyer, Professional Athlete,
Celebrity, Astronaut, Congressman,
Senator, President, Millionaire!
As faint as the wind, I heard this line,
"It's not your plan that matters, but Mine."

When I got older, I began to pray.
"Use my life, Lord, in any way."
But inside my heart He heard me say,
"Here's a list, God. Pick away."
Salesman, Manager, Counselor,
Engineer, Small Business Owner, Architect,
Teacher, Rancher, Middle Class.
Like the sweet sound of rain, I heard this line,
"It's not your plan that matters, but Mine."

Now that I'm weathered, I try to pray,
"Use my life, Lord, in any way."
And inside my heart He hears me say,
"Here's a list, God. Pick away."
Laborer, Minimum Wage Worker, Janitor,
Garbage Man, Groundskeeper, Unemployed,
Hungry, Homeless, Broke.
Like thunder in a storm I echo His line,
"It's not your plan that matters, but Mine."

Caffeinated Questions

1. Do you have a personal relationship with Jesus? How do you know?

2. If you're confident that you do have a personal relationship with Jesus, what areas of your life do you have trouble giving Him control over?

3. Why do you struggle giving Him control of these areas?

SURFING PRINCIPLES

4 Dreamer's Principles

Plan ambitiously
Prepare persistently
Persevere courageously
Accelerate toward fear

10 Trailblazer's Rhythms

 1. Practice blue-collar goal setting.

 2. Focus on the next small step.

 3. Celebrate short-term wins.

 4. Maintain momentum.

 5. Adjust as clarity presents.

 6. Maintain a manageable pace.

 7. Seize the moments.

 8. Don't journey alone.

 9. Overload.

 10. Prioritize paradoxically.

The Dreamer's Creed

I'll go where I'm scared to go,
I'll face what I'm scared to face,
I'll say what I'm scared to say,
To live the dream God has for me.

SURFING TERMS

Accelerate toward fear: Using your fears as guideposts to point you in the direction of the ambitious journey to which God is calling you

Blue-collar goal setting: An effective method of goal setting which helps you evaluate your activities through a simple grid of "stop, start, and keep" questions

Clarifying moments: Obstacles, setbacks, and defeats that happen as you pursue your God-inspired dream

Disbelievers: People who miss out on their potential because they tell themselves that pursuing ambitious dreams is immature or fanciful thinking

Dream door: The metaphorical door behind which we keep our ambitions and dreams; this door often becomes locked shut because of hurt, disappointment, or failure

Dream-door opener: People who inspire others to move away from the safe zone and begin pursuing God's ambitious calling

Effective dreamers: People who are courageously moving their God-inspired dreams forward and are experiencing satisfying results

Energizing passion: The passion behind the activity that gives you daily energy or re-energizes you when you're off track

Excuse makers: People who miss out on their potential because they are trapped in a cycle of disappointment and finger pointing

God-inspired dream: The ambitious pursuits that God specifically calls you toward in partnership with His unlimited power

LEAP: An acronym for learn your story, explore your uniqueness, aim for your God-inspired dream, and plan your next steps

Motivating impact zone: The people group or cause you naturally desire to impact with your life

Overload: The process of slowly and consistently elevating the stress level of an activity toward whatever goal you have in mind

Prioritize paradoxically: Becoming more effective by doing the opposite of what your mind, body, and emotions naturally want to do

Safe zone: The place people unknowingly go when trying to avoid potential disappointment, hurt, and failure; the place where ambitions die.

Safe-zoners: People who miss out on their potential because they aren't accelerating toward their fears

Short-term wins: Small victories and clarifying moments that are to be celebrated along the ambitious journey

Surfing the woods; surfing life: Pursuing the ambitious life effectively

Unique effect: The distinctive way you affect people when you interact with them

Unique story; God-inspired name: The word or phrase that summarizes the unique story of your life

Unique strengths: Those things that come naturally for you; the tools in your being that you rely on in order to accomplish a task or goal

Wanderers: People who miss out on their potential because they have trouble putting their God-inspired dreams into action

APPENDIX 1

Blue-Collar Goal Setting Worksheet

The Weekly "Big Three"

1. What progress did I make last week?
2. What step(s) will I take this week?
3. What fears do I need to walk into to make progress this week?

Momentum Changers

1. As it relates to managing self, what do I need to stop, start, and keep doing?

   Stop

   Start

   Keep

2. As it relates to managing relationships, what do I need to stop, start, and keep doing?

   Stop

   Start

   Keep

3. As it relates to managing problems and opportunities, what do I need to stop, start, and keep doing?

   Stop

   Start

   Keep

APPENDIX 2

Scripture Memory Suggestions

Walking in power

James 1:23–25
James 3:2–6
1 John 1:7
Hebrews 10:24–25
Hebrews 11:6
Luke 14:33
John 8:47
John 5:19
Matthew 22:37–38
John 14:21
John 15:4–5
Ephesians 4:29
Romans 12:1–2
Psalm 119:9–11
Joshua 1:8
James 3:16–18
Galatians 5:16

Strength to endure

James 1:2–4, 1:12
1 Corinthians 10:13
Romans 8:35, 8:38–39
Hebrews 12:1–3
2 Corinthians 4:16–18

Psalm 33:16–19
Psalm 37:4–7
Philippians 4:4–8
1 Peter 2:21–24

Real love

1 John 3:18–20
John 13:34–35
Hebrews 10:24–25
Matthew 7:12
1 Corinthians 13:4–8
Ephesians 5:25, 5:27–28

Your powerful position in Christ

1 Peter 2:9
Ephesians 3:20–21
2 Corinthians 12:9
1 Chronicles 29:11–12
Psalm 20:7
Ephesians 2:8–10
Romans 8:35, 8:38–39
Psalm 139:1–5

Living humbly

Philippians 2:3–4
James 4:6
Ephesians 2:8–10
Matthew 7:3–5
1 Peter 5:5–6
James 3:16–18
1 Corinthians 13:4–8

How to have a personal relationship with Christ

Romans 3:10
Romans 3:23
Romans 6:23
Romans 5:8
Romans 8:1
Romans 10:9

Fighting the enemy

Psalm 119:9–11
Ephesians 6:10–18

APPENDIX 3

The LEAP Profile

(refer to pages 150-164)

My God-inspired name (story) is:

My strengths are:

My energizing passion is:

My unique effect is:

My motivating impact zone is:

My calling is:

I am shaping the following God-inspired dreams:

1.

2.

3.

4.

APPENDIX 4

How to know Jesus Christ

If you are interested in entering into a relationship with Jesus Christ, consider this.

- **The Bible says we are all sinners.**

  "For everyone has sinned; we all fall short of God's glorious standard." (Ro. 3:23, NLT)

  "No one is righteous—not even one." (Ro. 3:10, NLT)

- **Because of our sin we are deserving of death, but the good news is God desires to pardon us.**

  "For the wages of sin is death, but the free gift of God is eternal life through Christ Jesus our Lord." (Ro. 6:23, NLT)

- **The Bible says that God loved us so much He sent Jesus to pay our penalty for sin.**

  "But God showed his great love for us by sending Christ to die for us while we were still sinners." (Ro. 5:8, NLT)

- **If we belong to Jesus we are no longer under the penalty of death.**

  "So now there is no condemnation for those who belong to Christ Jesus." (Ro. 8:1, NLT)

- **God offers this gift of salvation to all who sincerely put their faith in Christ Jesus.**

"If you confess with your mouth that Jesus is Lord and believe in your heart that God raised him from the dead, you will be saved." (Ro. 10:9, NLT)

"For God loved the world so much that he gave his one and only Son, so that everyone who believes in him will not perish but have eternal life." (John 3:16, NLT)

- **If you want to begin this new relationship with Christ, start with this simple prayer.**

    Lord Jesus, I know I am a sinner and do not deserve eternal life. But I believe You died and rose from the grave to purchase a place in heaven for me. Jesus, come into my life, take control of my life, forgive my sins, and save me. I am now placing my trust in You alone for my salvation, and I accept your free gift of eternal life.

- **If this prayer is the sincere desire of your heart, look at the promise of Jesus.**

    "I assure you: Anyone who believes has eternal life." (John 6:47, HCSB)

If you, having read this, trusted Jesus for eternal life, please let us know. You can contact us at www.surfthewoods.com. We want to rejoice in what God has done in your life and help you to grow spiritually.

If you would like more information about entering into a personal relationship with Jesus Christ, check out www.juststopandthink.com.

What people are saying about

SURF THE WOODS

"Every man longs to play his part in the great adventure. Holt Condren has a unique gift to challenge your men through biblical truth and life stories."

Bill Elliff

Sr. Teaching Pastor of The Summit Church, North Little Rock, AR, author and Pastor/Church Director of OneCry! A Nationwide Call for Spiritual Awakening

"It is awesome to partner with Holt over the years and to see how the principles laid out in Surf the Woods can transform lives. He has used these same principles to help us at FCA impact millions of people each year through resource and Bible distribution."

Dan Britton

Executive Vice President of Fellowship of Christian Athletes, Kansas City, MO and author and editor of 11 books including WisdomWalks

"Holt does a wonderful job of inspiring men to live a life of significance, but more important, he utilizes the principles found in God's word to instruct them on how to do it. He has a gift of using life events to engage, challenge and instruct men on reaching their potential for which God has called them."

Randy Cameron

Pastor of Church Growth, First Baptist Church, Bentonville, AR

"Holt has been a great inspiration to my congregation, challenging and encouraging us to grow beyond our current places of comfort. I can think of no other person or message that I would recommend more strongly than that of Holt's heart message delivered through *Surf the Woods*."

Chris Sims

Sr. Teaching Pastor of Pilgrims Rest Baptist Church, Batesville, AR

BRING *Surf the Woods* TO YOUR GROUP

INSPIRING TALKS

Great for men's events (breakfasts, retreats, etc.), church services, youth retreats, or corporate meetings.

CONFERENCES & RETREATS

Energizing two-day conferences available as an onsite conference or an offsite retreat.

ADVENTURE TRIPS

Let us customize an outdoor adventure for you next corporate outing or church retreat.

CONSULTING SERVICES

Are you or your organization having trouble achieving the level of effectiveness you expect? Holt is available for customized one-on-one or group coaching.

SurftheWoods.com

CPSIA information can be obtained
at www.ICGtesting.com
Printed in the USA
LVOW12s1423110318
569456LV00001B/132/P